NOTES ON THINGS KOREAN

NOTES

on

THINGS KOREAN

Suzanne Crowder Han

HOLLYM

Elizabeth, NJ · Seoul

Notes on Things Korean

First published in 1995
Sixth printing, 2002 ˙
by Hollym International Corp.
18 Donald Place, Elizabeth, NJ 07208, U.S.A.
Tel: (908)353-1655   Fax: (908)353-0255
http://www.hollym.com

Published simultaneously in Korea
by Hollym Corporation; Publishers
13-13 Kwanchol-dong, Chongno-gu, Seoul 110-111, Korea
Tel: (02)735-7551~4   Fax: (02)730-5149
http://www.hollym.co.kr

Hardbound edition ISBN: 1-56591-019-2
Paperbound edition ISBN: 1-56591-036-2
Library of Congress Catalog Card No.: 95-76496

Illustrations by Kahyon Kim

Printed in Korea

Preface

This is a compilation of notes on a wide spectrum of things Korean. It is for anyone interested in Korean life, thought and culture.

I first felt the need for such a book when I was working as an editorial consultant for an agency producing English language books about Korea. The text for this book grew out of the many notes on "Things Korean" that I made to help me in my work. Although a lot of research went into compiling the notes, I am no expert and the notes are by no means authoritative.

Of course, there is no end to the topics that could go into this book. I have tried to include topics that provide insight into Korean beliefs, customs, practices and ways of life and are either unique to Korea, of historical significance, or commonly encountered. I also included a selection of prominent personalities who contributed greatly to Korean cultural and social development, a selection of famous monuments and places of interest, and a selection of games and sports. Some of the entries were taken from other books or articles I have written.

Except for a few names, a slightly modified version of the McCune-Reischauer system of romanizing has been used for Korean terms. An introduction is included to provide some background about Korea and Korean culture and in the back of the book is a bibliography of resources and a glossary of Korean terms. I would like to thank Mr. Chu Shin-won, Ms. Kang Sue-jung of Hollym and Mrs. Uhm Kyoung-hee, who have been patient, understanding and supportive; Mrs. Elizabeth Kraft Lee and Mr. Han Nae-bok, two former colleagues who have always been a source of advice, information and inspiration; and, Mrs. Kim Miza, a dear friend who has helped me in too many ways to enumerate.

SCH

Contents

10 ○ *Contents*

GAMES AND SPORTS

MISCELLANEOUS

Introduction

The Republic of Korea is located on the Korean Peninsula which arches a little over 600 miles (965 kilometers) southward and slightly eastward from the southeastern corner of the Asian continent. Bordered by Manchuria and Russia to the north, China to the west across the Yellow Sea, and Japan to the east and south across the Sea of Japan and Strait of Tsushima, it was a strategic land bridge via which peoples and cultural developments from the Asian continent reached the islands of the Pacific in ancient times.

Korea's total land area including some 3,000 islands is approximately 38,655 square miles (99,117 square kilometers). It is a mountainous land embroidered with rivers. The eastern part is more rugged than the western as it has several towering mountain ranges, deep valleys and almost no coastal plains. The western part has most of the large rivers and the richer alluvial lands. The coastline is indented with bays, inlets and harbors and the tides rise to incredible heights, the world's second highest in Inch'ŏn.

The climate ranges from cold and dry in the north to almost semitropical in some southern areas with the main precipitation occurring during the steamy summer months of July and August. Spring, which is short and mild, and autumn, which is long and cool, are the most pleasant and colorful of Korea's four seasons.

Koreans speak their own language and use their own alphabet. They are descendants of Mongol tribes that emigrated to the Korean Peninsula about twenty-four centuries before Christ and brought a strong belief in animism with them. However, legend has it that they are descended from a man-god named Tan-gun who founded Chosŏn, Land of Morning Calm, in 2333 B.C.

Tribal communities rose and fell from around that time until three kingdoms—Shilla, Koguryŏ and Paekche—came into existence and began to flourish around 60 B.C. Although politically separate, the three kingdoms were related ethnically and linguistically. They maintained contact with each other, either in alliances with each other against China, who established commanderies in the northern part of the peninsula, or at war with each other allied with China. Shilla, with its capital at Sŏrabŏl, today's Kyŏngju, consolidated the other two kingdoms to create the first unified state on the peninsula in A.D. 668 and inaugurated a golden age of art.

In 918 Shilla was replaced by a new kingdom called Koryŏ, from which the name "Korea" is derived. During Koryŏ, laws were codified and a civil service system was instituted. Buddhism, which came to Korea via China in A.D. 372, printing and the arts, especially celadon ceramics, flourished. Movable metal type began to be used for printing in 1234, two centuries before Gutenberg. However, Koryŏ suffered several Mongol invasions in the thirteenth century that eventually led to its downfall in 1392.

Koryŏ was replaced by the Chosŏn Kingdom founded by an ex-Koryŏ general named Yi Sŏng-gye, or T'aejo as he is known by his dynastic title. The Yi Dynasty founded by Yi Sŏng-gye produced twenty-six monarchs who ruled Chosŏn from Hanyang, today's Seoul, until the country was annexed by Japan in 1910.

The early Chosŏn kings made Neo-Confucianism the official belief system in order to counter Buddhism and appropriate the great wealth accumulated by Buddhist temples. Neo-Confucianism made filial piety the ultimate social virtue, requiring ancestral rites be the most important religious ceremony in the household and stressing propriety in social relationships. The Chosŏn Kingdom redistributed land, expanded the aristocracy, and increasingly relied on the use of examinations for qualifying individuals for important positions.

During the five hundred years of the Chosŏn Kingdom, contacts with countries other than China were largely discouraged and international trade was limited to exchanging native products for luxury goods. When Japanese and Western traders arrived in the late nineteenth century, Chosŏn rulers could see little advantage in opening the country to trade with other countries and thus earned the country the nickname the "Hermit Kingdom." Entrenched in a Confucian and China-centered world view, the Chosŏn Kingdom was ill-prepared to deal with foreign demands for diplomatic and trade relations and to meet the threat of a modernizing Japan. Japan's victories in the 1894-95 Sino-Japanese War and 1904-05 Russo-Japanese War made it the unchallenged military power in Northeast Asia and the Chosŏn Kingdom became vulnerable to Japan's desire for empire. The kingdom finally fell in 1910 and was annexed by Japan.

For thirty-five years the Japanese ruled Korea as a colony but failed in their attempts at complete assimilation. During the occupation, Koreans founded an independence movement to oppose Japanese rule and Koreans outside the country established a government in exile in Shanghai, China.

With the 1945 Allied victory over Japan in World War II, Korea was liberated from Japanese rule but arbitrarily divided along the thirty-eighth parallel to facilitate the surrender of Japanese forces; the United States was to accept the surrender of Japanese forces south of the line, and the Soviet Union those north of the line. In 1947, the United Nations resolved to hold supervised general elections in both halves of the peninsula but the offer was rejected in the northern half. The Soviet Union set up a communist regime in the north called the Democratic People's Republic of Korea, or North Korea as it is more commonly known. In 1948 a national election was held in the southern half of the peninsula that resulted in the establishment of the Republic of Korea, or South Korea as it is popularly called.

Two years later, on June 25, 1950, North Korea invaded South Korea. The United Nations reacted swiftly to aid the South, sending armed forces and other forms of assistance from sixteen United Nations members. The three-year conflict that ensued brought massive destruction and complete social disruption before it was brought to a cease-fire in 1953.

The Republic of Korea has since developed into a newly industrializing nation.

Chronology

2333 B.C.	Tan-gun founds Old Chosŏn
57 B.C.	Shilla Kingdom emerges
37 B.C.	Koguryŏ Kingdom emerges
18 B.C.	Paekche Kingdom emerges
372 A.D.	Buddhism introduced to Koguryŏ via China
527	Buddhism sanctioned in Shilla
660	Paekche falls
668	Koguryŏ falls
670	Shilla repulses T'ang forces, unifies peninsula
918	Koryŏ Kingdom founded
935	Shilla falls to Koryŏ
957	Civil examination system instituted
1231-73	Mongol invasions
1234	Movable metal type invented
1392	Chosŏn Kingdom supersedes Koryŏ
1446	Korean alphabet invented
1592-98	Japanese invasions
1627-36	Manchu invasions
1876	Trade treaty signed with Japan; end of national isolation policy
1897	Taehan Empire proclaimed
1910	Annexation by Japan
1919	March First Independence Movement
1945-48	Liberation from Japanese rule Joint U.S.-U.S.S.R. occupation Establishment of the Democratic People's Republic of Korea and the Republic of Korea
1950-53	Korean War

BELIEFS AND CUSTOMS

Ancestral Rites, *Chesa*

The Confucian rituals or ceremonies through which Koreans pay homage to their ancestors *(chosang)* are collectively known as *chesa*. The rites are an integral part of the Korean ethos which emphasizes a vertical order from the eldest down to the youngest including the dead down to the descendants. The rites are a reaffirmation of blood kinship between the living and the dead through which family ties are strengthened among the living.

There are basically three types of *chesa: kije*, or death anniversary commemoration, which is performed at midnight on the eve of the ancestor's death day; *ch'arye*, or holiday commemoration, which is performed in the morning on certain holidays; and, *myoje*, or grave-side commemoration, which is performed when one visits the grave *(myo)*.

The *kije* and *ch'arye* involve the offering of food and drink to the ancestors. The ceremonies may vary slightly from family to family and region to region but there are some basic rules for the arrangement of the ritual table *(ch'arye sang)* and the process of ritual performance. Certain foods are placed on the east side of the table and certain foods on the west; for example, red fruit is placed on the east side of the table and white on the west. The row of food closest to the officiants holds fruit, the next row, vegetables, the next, thick soups, and a variety of meat and fish, and, at the far back, bowls of rice and soup and spoons and chopsticks. In front of the table is a table for an incense burner and in front of it, a tray for wine.

The ceremony begins when the eldest male in the family kneels down at the small table to burn incense. He stands up, bows deeply, head to floor, twice and then kneels again and pours three cups of wine into a bowl to symbolize the ancestor's descent to the offering table. Everyone bows three times—two head-to-floor bows, and a light one, that is, bending the upper body in a fifteen degree angle.

The eldest son then offers a cup of wine after rotating it three times in the incense smoke. He is usually assisted by a younger brother who pours the wine while he holds the cup. After the wine is offered, the helper moves the chopsticks to a plate of food. All the participants bow as before. Then the next eldest male, and the next down to the youngest offers a cup of wine, repeating the actions of the eldest. Some families offer only three cups of wine and some more. Once the wine offering is completed, the spoon is placed in the rice bowl and the men leave the room or turn their backs to let the ancestor feast at will. After a few minutes, the men return and the soup is removed and a bowl of water put in its place. The participants bow as before and that concludes the ritual. The food is then served to all the family.

The *kije* is traditionally performed at midnight on the eve of the ancestor's death day but many families now perform it in the more convenient early evening hours. Only one ancestor or an ancestral couple is honored in the *kije*.

Ch'arye honors all ancestors for four generations back. The food and procedures follow the pattern of *kije* with a few minor variations. *Ch'arye* is performed in the early morning and holiday specialties replace rice and soup. Most families perform *ch'arye* twice a year, on New Year's and Ch'usŏk, but some also perform it on Hanshik, the one hundred fifth day after the winter solstice, and on Tano, the fifth day of the fifth lunar month (*see* entries in Special Days).

Myoje, or grave-side rituals, are simpler than *kije* and *ch'arye.* Only a few dishes are offered with wine.

The tangible object of veneration in the *kije* and *ch'arye* rites is a wooden ancestor tablet called *shinju* or *wip'ae* or a disposable paper substitute called *chibang.* Most families today use the latter. The ancestor's name, title and place of origin *(pon)* are written in black ink on the paper and it is attached to the wall or to a folding screen behind the table-*cum*-altar. The paper is burned at the end of the rite.

Birth

The birth of a child, particularly a son, is regarded by Koreans as a highly fortunate event on which great importance is placed owing to the necessity for the continuity of ancestor veneration, an underlying principle of the Korean system of ethics. In the hope of being blessed with a son, many women still pray and make offerings to the Birth Grandmother (Samshin Halmŏni), the Mountain Spirit (Sanshin), the Seven Star Spirit (Ch'ilsŏng, or the Big Dipper), the Buddha, phallic-shaped rocks, and trees and rocks that are considered sacred. The Birth Grandmother is considered especially important as she provides for the birth of a child and its growth and rearing. The Mongolian spot, or blue mark, which is usually present on the buttocks of Oriental infants is said to be the place where the Birth Grandmother slaps the child to bring it to life.

To announce the birth of a child, a straw rope, called *kŭmjul*, meaning "forbidding rope," is hung across the gate to the house, a custom that is no longer widely practiced. It is kept up for twenty-one days to frighten evil spirits away and to warn people not to enter because of the presence of a newborn, which, before the advent of modern medicine, was probably conducive to the child's well-being. The rope is usually intertwined with pine branches, charcoal and red peppers to indicate a male and with pine branches and charcoal to indicate a female.

Birthdays, *Saeng-il*

Hundredth Day, *Paegil* On the one hundredth day of a child's birth, *paegil*, a small feast is held to celebrate the child having survived this difficult period of life. If the child is sick at the time, no feast is held for fear of bringing bad luck upon it. Before the feasting begins, an offering of soup and rice is made to the Birth Grandmother (Samshin Halmŏni) and red bean cakes are placed at the four compass points within the house to prevent disaster and bring the child good luck and happiness. Rice cakes are sent to as many people as possible to share the happiness of the occasion and the recipients return the containers with skeins of thread or yarn symbolizing longevity or rice or money symbolizing wealth.

First Birthday, *Tol* A larger feast is held on the child's first birthday, or *tol*. The highlight of the *tol* celebration is a ritual by which the child foretells its future. The child is dressed in a traditional Korean costume with rainbow-striped sleeves. Males wear a vest, topcoat and hood that are decorated with auspicious symbols over their clothes and females wear an overgarment resembling a ceremonial robe of ancient court ladies and a silk hat. The child is seated before a table of various foods and objects such as thread, books, writing brushes, ink, money, arrows or daggers, uncooked rice, needles and scissors, depending on the sex of the child. The object the child picks up first is believed to foretell its future: a writing brush or book, a scholar; an arrow or dagger, a military officer; money or rice, wealthy. Thread is used for both males and females because it symbolizes long life. Guests usually bring gifts of money, clothes or gold rings and are given rice cakes on departing to bring the child long life and happiness.

Sixtieth Birthday, *Hwan-gap* The sixtieth birthday, *hwan-gap,* is especially important for it marks the completion of the full cycle of sixty years (*see* Lunar Calendar in Lifestyle), a great accomplishment before the advent of modern medicine when living to fifty was even rare. It is customary at this time for children to honor their parents with a large feast and much merrymaking.

Dressed in traditional Korean dress, the parents sit at a table laden with special foods to receive obeisance and wine from all their children and grandchildren and their spouses, in order by age. After the direct descendants have performed these ritual bows and offerings, the honoree's younger siblings and their spouses and children, friends and guests pay their respects in the same manner. If there is an older family member, he or she is seated at a similar table and receives bows and wine first. While these rituals are performed, those who have already paid their respect are served food and drink.

In the past, music was usually played and professional entertainers sang songs urging people to drink. Guests competed in composing poetry or songs to celebrate the occasion and family members indulged in various activities to make their parents feel young, often dressing as small children and dancing and singing songs.

In the past, the years after the sixtieth birthday were considered extra years and each was celebrated, albeit not as lavishly. The seventieth birthday, *kohŭi*, meaning "old and rare," was celebrated on the same scale as the *hwan-gap*.

Buddhism, Pulgyo

Pulgyo, as Buddhism is called in Korean, was introduced to Korea in the fourth century A.D., first in Koguryŏ by a Chinese monk in 372 and then in Paekche by an Indian monk who came via China in 384. The new faith spread rapidly through the two kingdoms as it apparently received royal patronage and by the sixth century monks and religious artisans were journeying to Japan with Buddhist scriptures and artifacts. However, it was rejected by the Shilla government until around 527 when the royal family adopted it as the state religion because of alleged miracles performed by saintly monks. It became a powerful influence and eventually an integral part of Korean culture. It reached its peak in the Koryŏ Kingdom (928-1392), with monks, who were well-educated and thus able to act as scribes and advisors, exerting a powerful influence in national affairs, even overruling royal decrees and leading social and political revolutions. However, it eventually degenerated because of the luxury of temple life and the worldly ambitions of corrupt monks who meddled in politics and thus was blamed for Koryŏ's decline. With the establishment of the Chosŏn Kingdom in 1392, it fell into disfavor and was suppressed in favor of Confucianism.

Buddhism first reached Korea in the form called Mahayana, or the Great Vehicle, but eventually all the forms which were popular in China during the T'ang period were transmitted to Korea, mainly by Korean monks who studied there. The most influential were Avatamsaka Buddhism, which based its teachings on the sutra of the same name; Esoteric Buddhism, which emphasized the importance of ritual; Amitahba or Pure Land Buddhism, which stressed prayer (*yŏmbul*) as the means of redemption; and, Meditation Buddhism, which emphasized meditation and is known as Sŏn in Korean and Zen in Japanese. Other forms were later introduced but in the twelfth century a Korean monk named Chinul (1158-1210: *see* Chinul in Historic Figures) developed a new form, Chogye-jong, emphasizing constant discipline, prayer, the study of sutras and meditation. The Chogye-jong School has been the predominant form since about 1200 and controls most of the temples and monasteries in Korea.

As Korean Buddhism developed through the ages, it blended well with native beliefs and other religions and developed an elaborate and complex hierarchy of deities, saints and guardians. It also stimulated the development of the arts, especially architecture, ceramics, sculpture, metalwork, wood carving, painting and printing.

Korean Buddhists believe in individual immortal souls, a vicarious salvation through Amitahba Buddha, reincarnation, confession, hell, and heaven, the Western Pure Land and Nirvana. They believe that to pass from this world of misery to that of heaven the six virtues of charity, morality, patience, energy, contemplation, and wisdom must be perfected. And they believe in a host of Buddhas (*Puch'ŏ*) and Boddhisattvas (*Posal*) and practice many forms of sacrifice to them. (*see* Buddhist Deities in this chapter; Buddhist Temples in Famous Places and Monuments)

Buddhist Deities

Buddhas, *Puch'ŏ* Sakyamuni (Sŏkkamoni bul) is one of the most popular Buddhas *(puch'ŏ)* in Korea. Sakyamuni is the title given to the historical Buddha, Siddhartha Gautama, and means "Sage of the Sakyas." If the main sanctum of a temple (*see* Buddhist Temples in Famous Places and Monuments) contains an image of Sakyamuni, the building is called Taeungjŏn or Taeungbojŏn.

Sakyamuni rarely appears alone. He is usually at the center of a trinity, flanked by Bodhisattvas, historical personages or other Buddhas. He is most often flanked by Amitahba (Amit'a bul), the Buddha of Infinite Light, and Bhaisajyaguru (Yaksayŏrye bul), the Buddha of Medicine; his two favorite disciples, Ananda (Ananda) and Kasyapa (Kasŏp), representing intellect and experience; Maitreya (Mirŭk bul), the Coming or Future Buddha, and Dipamkara (Chehwagalla), the first of the earthly Buddhas; Manjusri (Munsu posal), the Bodhisattva of Wisdom, and Samantabhadra (Pŏhyŏn posal), the Bodhisattva of Power and Love; or Vairocana (Pirojana bul), the Spreading the Light of Buddhist Truth Buddha, and Bhaisajyaguru.

One of the easiest ways to identify an image is through the mudra (*suin*), hand gestures signifying powers and special actions. The Touching the Ground or Calling the Earth to Witness mudra is the mudra most often associated with images of Sakyamuni. In seated figures, one hand hangs over the knee, palm inward, pointing with one finger, or all, toward the ground, symbolizing Sakyamuni's lordship over the earth.

Amitahba is the Buddha of Infinite Light who governs the Pure Land, or Western Paradise as it is sometimes called. If he is the major image in the main sanctum, the hall is called Kŭngnakchŏn. However, he rarely appears alone. He is usually flanked by Avalokitesvara (Kwanseŭm posal), the Bodhisattva of Mercy, and Mahasthamaprapta (Taeseji posal), the Bodhisattva of Power. When standing, Amitahba usually holds his left hand palm outward in a gesture of offering and when seated, the left hand is usually held palm upward in the lap. The right hand is

raised, granting an absence of fear, with the thumb touching the index, middle or ring finger to form a circle representing the perfection of wisdom. The Touching the Ground mudra is also associated with this Buddha who vowed to save all who call on him by admitting them to his Pure Land where they will meet no obstacles to achieving enlightenment.

Bhaisajyaguru, the Medicine Buddha, the Healer, generally has no attending figures, is usually white instead of gold, and holds a medicine bowl. The bowl is usually held in both hands but sometimes in only the left, in which case the right is in the Absence of Fear mudra. Bhaisajyaguru provides relief from disease, misfortune and ignorance, the ill to which man is most susceptible.

Maitreya, the Future Buddha, is easily identified for he is usually depicted sitting pensively with legs half crossed. The posture indicates that he is sitting in his paradise, Tusita, preparing to be born in this world for the salvation of living things.

Vairocana, who spreads the light of Buddhist truth, is the embodiment of truth and knowledge. He is easy to recognize because usually the left index finger, representing the world of sentient beings, is held by the closed fist of the right, representing the protection of the world by Buddha. He is also represented with hands joined palm to palm; the right hand enclosing the left hand closed in a fist; and, the fingers crossed over one another and the thumbs up. He is often enshrined in his own building, Pirochŏn, in which case there are no attendants.

Six Mudras

Bodhisattvas, *Posal* Avalokitesvara, the Bodhisattva of Mercy, or

Kwanseŭm posal in Korean, has many forms but is usually identifiable by the small figure of Amitahba Buddha in the diadem
she wears and the vase and willow spray she holds. The vase
contains the nectar of compassion and the willow spray represents her ability to sprinkle the nectar on the afflicted. She is
often depicted with nine heads or eleven, and with numerous
eyes and limbs. Some images have a mustache, which is perhaps
a vestige from very ancient times when this Buddha was first
depicted as male.

Ksitigarba, the Bodhisattva of Hell, who is known as Chijang
posal in Korean, is enshrined in a building called Myŏngbujŏn.
He is accompanied by two attendants and ten judges who determine one's fate after death. He is easily identified for he is usually
depicted as bald or with closely cropped hair and holding a staff.
The judges are usually in statue form and each stands in front of
a colorful painting of the territory he governs. Funerals are held
in the Myŏngbujŏn and pictures and memorial tablets of
deceased persons are installed in it and services conducted for
them.

Other Deities Ch'ilsŏng, the Seven Star Spirit, which has its
roots in Taoism and Shamanism, is often seen in the form of a
painting on one of the inner side walls of the Myŏngbujŏn. The
colorful painting contains many festive scenes and figures and is
identifiable by the seven Buddhas in a row at the top. Ch'ilsŏng
is highly revered because the Great Bear Constellation, the Big
Dipper, is visible year round. It is believed to control good and
bad fortune. It is presumed to have become incorporated in Buddhism as it spread through the Korean peninsula because it was
viewed as a manifestation of the compassionate Buddha.

Sanshin, the shamanist-inspired Mountain Spirit, is usually
enshrined in the form of a painting in a small hall on a slope
behind the main hall or with a small altar in one of the large
halls. The Sanshin is easy to identify for he is usually depicted as
an old bearded man with a tiger.

Toksŏng, the Lonely Saint, is often enshrined in the form of a
painting in a small hall with the Sanshin, the Ch'ilsŏng, or both,

or in a hall of its own. Toksŏng is easily identified because he is usually accompanied by a young boy holding a fan, a platter of fruit, or tea.

Guardians In small temples, Vajras (Kŭmgang shinjang) are often painted on the doors of the Ilchumun, the gate that leads to the temple grounds and usually bears the name of the temple. These fierce-looking deities send forth deadly rays of light, one from the mouth and one from the nostrils, to prevent evil spirits from entering the temple. As the mouth is the door to the face and thus to the body, the open and closed mouths of the two gods symbolically indicate that the temple is protected whether the gate is opened or closed.

In large temples, one must pass through a second, larger gate that usually houses huge statues or paintings of Lokapala, the Four Heavenly Kings, which are called Sach'ŏnwang in Korean. The fierce-looking rulers of the four cardinal points protect the temple by crushing the enemies of Buddhism under their feet.

Dhrtarastra (Chiguk ch'ŏnwang), the Guardian of the East, has blue skin, a closed mouth, a clenched left hand, and holds a sword in the right hand which he can replicate to outnumber opponents. Virudhaka (Chŭngjang ch'ŏnwang), the Guardian of the South, has red skin, angry eyes, and holds a jewel in the left hand and a dragon in the right. Virupaska (Kwangmok ch'ŏnwang), the Guardian of the West, has white skin, an open mouth, and holds a three-part pagoda, which represents the earth, heaven, and cosmos, in the left hand and a forked lance in the right. Vaisrana (Tamun ch'ŏnwang), the Guardian of the North, has black skin, bared teeth, and holds a lute with both hands.

Changsŭng, Spirit Posts

Changsŭng is the common name for the sometimes grotesque, sometimes humorous posts that stand in pairs at the entrances to villages and temples or at a turn in a path. The purported function of the posts is complex but it is basically to protect the village from evil spirits and thereby ensure the peace and prosperity of all that reside therein. With time, the distance between villages came to be measured from the *changsŭng* of one village to the *changsŭng* of another.

Changsŭng vary in shape and material according to locale; wooden poles are common in the central region of the country whereas stone posts are more common in the southern region. They are called *changsŭng* in Kyŏnggi-do, *susal* in Ch'ungch'ŏng-do, *poksu* in Kyŏngsang-do and Chŏlla-do, and *harubang* on Chejudo Island. "Great General Under Heaven" is usually inscribed in Chinese characters on the male *changsŭng*, and "Female General Under Ground," on the female.

It was common practice, and still is in some villages, to hold periodic rites to honor the tutelary spirits that reside in the posts. These involved the offering of food and drink which was enjoyed by all the villagers after the completion of the rites. Similar rituals were also held before the *changsŭng* to pray for a bountiful harvest or for protection from a calamity or disease that had befallen a neighboring village.

The erecting and replacing of wooden *changsŭng* was done in lunar leap months, which occur every three years, and involved several steps and rituals, including a rite to honor the Sanshin (Mountain Spirit). A village meeting was held to choose a man to lead the rituals; he was chosen from a group who had not seen a dead body or the blood of an animal during a certain period of time and who were considered lucky. People were also designated to clean the area where the posts were to be erected, to prepare the food offerings, to select and cut down the trees to be used and to do the carving and erecting. The *changsŭng* had to be made and raised all in the same day; this included the cutting of the trees, usually pine but sometimes chestnut or alder, and the carving and/or painting of the faces.

When *changsŭng* began to be erected is not known for sure. But historical records show that they were being erected in the mid eighth century.

Ch'ŏndogyo, Religion of the Heavenly Way

An indigenous Korean religion, Ch'ŏndogyo, the Religion of the Heavenly Way, upholds a similar concept of god as Christianity. However, its god, called Hanullim, is not a being that resides elsewhere and is to be revered or dreaded; it is to be discovered within oneself. Ch'ŏndogyo teaches that Hanullim and man are not separate beings but are one. In other words, that man is Hanullim.

Ch'ŏndogyo was first founded under the name Tonghak (Eastern Learning) in 1860 by Ch'oe Che-u (1824-1864), a petty aristocrat-scholar from Kyŏngju who was disillusioned with the social climate of the times. Ch'oe took the basic precepts of Confucianism, Buddhism and Taoism to form the religion in order to oppose Catholicism which he saw as representative of the Western learning and ideas that were threatening the already staggering Chosŏn Kingdom. Ch'ŏndogyo was thus born, in part, out of a protest against the infringement of Korea's political freedom and sovereignty by Western nations.

Ch'oe acquired his great awakening in the Heavenly Way in 1860 after many years of study and meditation. He immediately began to preach his beliefs and soon gained a large following, especially among rural people who were mercilessly extorted by corrupt government officials. However, he was viewed as a threat by the authorities because his theory of the unity of man and God promoted an equality of all humans that transcended social class or status. He was executed in 1864 on charges of misleading people and sowing discord in society. His followers, however, sought the realization of his ideas through a popular uprising in 1894. It was quickly put down and the movement went underground until 1905 when Son Pyŏng-hŭi proclaimed its revitalization under the name Ch'ŏndogyo.

Confucianism, Yugyo

The exact date Confucianism, or Yugyo as it is called in Korean, entered Korea is not known. However, evidence shows that Confucian rites were performed by early tribal states and the Shilla, Koguryŏ and Paekche kingdoms all left records which show an early existence of Confucian influence. With time Confucianism exerted a strong influence on social and governmental institutions, but it was not until the establishment of the Chosŏn Kingdom and its ousting of Buddhism from political influence in the late fourteenth century that Confucianism, rather Neo-Confucianism, was elevated to the status of a state cult. Education in the Chinese classics, particularly the writings of Confucius, whom Koreans call Kongja, became the sole basis of education and erudition represented the only path to social and political success. State examinations, called *kwagŏ* (*see* entry in Miscellaneous), determined the criteria for advancement of the scholar-official, the only career which a man of talent and breeding could honorably pursue. The *kwagŏ* system was practiced until 1894.

Although Confucianism no longer dictates the government system, it thrives more in Korea than in any other Asian nation, including China. Its basic values and premises still dominate the lives of Koreans. Ancestor veneration continues to be practiced in much the same way it has been for centuries (*see* Ancestral Rites in this chapter). Deference to age, respect for elders and superiors, and responsibility toward family are well practiced ideals. *Sŏkchŏn* (*see* Rites for Confucius in this chapter), a memorial ceremony honoring Confucius and his disciples, is held twice a year, in spring and fall, at Munmyo, the Temple of Confucius (*see* entry in Famous Places and Monuments).

Fortunetelling, *Chŏm*

Koreans, education and religious affiliation notwithstanding, consult fortunetellers, or *chŏmjangi*, for such important matters as names for children, proper marriage partners, prospective schools, career changes and suitable days for weddings, funerals, traveling and moving.

Many methods of fortunetelling including face and palm reading are used in Korea but the most popular method is *saju p'alcha*, or Four Pillars, Eight Characters. The equivalent of the Western horoscope, it is based on the lunar calendar (*see* entry in Lifestyle) and Oriental zodiac (*see* entry in this chapter) and involves a complicated system of calculations based on one's *saju*, that is, the year, month, day and hour of one's birth, and one's *p'alcha*, four pairs of cyclical characters associated with one's *saju*, all collectively known as *saju p'alcha*. One's *saju p'alcha* is of course unchanging but it is effected by the horoscopic properties of each year and each changing hour, day and month.

Using one's *saju p'alcha*, the fortuneteller, who is usually steeped in Chinese cosmology, consults ancient books of divination which were based on the *I-ching, The Book of Changes*, the first of Confucius's canons which gives insight into the cosmic and social changes that affect man.

The New Year season is traditionally a time for checking one's fortune and fortunetellers with a book called *T'ojŏng pigyŏl* are a common sight at markets, street corners, bus stops and other places where people tend to gather. *T'ojŏng pigyŏl (T'ojŏng's Secret)* is said to have been written by Yi Chi-ham (1517-78), a Confucian scholar whose penname was T'ojŏng. However, many scholars believe it was written by someone else using Yi's name because they do not believe that Yi, a scholar of Chinese classics, would have written such an unorthodox and heretical treatise.

Funerals, *Changrye*

Traditionally, Korean funerals *(changrye)* were held three, five, seven or nine days after the death of a person, depending on the person's social status—the more prominent the deceased, the longer the interval. Today most Korean funerals are held on the third day after death.

On the day before the funeral, an altar table is set up. A screen, or *pyŏngp'ung* (*see* entry in Arts and Crafts), is placed behind the table. A picture of the deceased is placed on the table and leaned against the screen. The altar is set with the first food offering.

After the altar is set up, the body of the deceased is washed and dressed in burial clothes, bound with rope, and placed in the coffin. Burial clothes are often purchased well in advance of need because preparing burial clothes for one's parents in advance is considered an act of filial piety on the part of adult children.

Once the body is placed in the coffin, the family members, including sons- and daughters-in-law, don mourning clothes made of bleached hemp cloth *(sambe)*. Though the men have been receiving condolence bearers, they now receive them in a more formal manner and the condolence bearers bow to the picture on the altar table before greeting the mourners. It is customary for condolence bearers to give money in an envelope. It is also customary for the family of the deceased to serve the condolence bearers food and drink and they may stay throughout the night to keep the mourners company.

The funeral procession begins with the removal of the coffin to the bier. A colorful catafalque was traditionally used to carry the coffin to the grave site but nowadays a special bus is usually used to transport both the coffin and the mourners to the grave site.

The carrying of the bier to the grave site was done with much fanfare in the past. The procession was usually led by men carrying funeral banners and burning incense and there was usually one man ringing a bell and singing in a deep, mournful voice. The bier came next followed by the eldest son, the other family members, relatives and friends. On arrival at the grave site, which would have been chosen by a geomancer (*see* Geomancy in this chapter) and dug to his specifications, the coffin was removed from the bier and lowered into the pit. Clay was packed around the coffin and then covered with dirt. The mourners stamped and danced on the grave to pack the earth in an effort to prevent water seepage. A round mound of earth was made over the grave and later sodded. This type of traditional funeral may still be encountered in the countryside, but is rare in cities.

After the burial, the mourning clothes are put away for use in future memorial services for the deceased. However, in the past it was customary for the children of the deceased to wear mourning clothes and refrain from any merriment for three years and some children even resided in a hut beside the grave. It was customary, and still is with some families, to offer meals to the deceased at the altar-table three times a day for a month and then to offer only a morning meal on the first and fifteenth day of every month for a year.

Many of these practices have disappeared while others have been greatly modified or simplified to suit today's way of life. For funerals nowadays, male mourners tend to wear black garments with armbands and legbands, and sometimes caps, of hemp cloth and female mourners, white hemp or rough cotton *hanbok* (*see* Dress in Lifestyle). For the three-month mourning period, men pin small bows of hemp cloth on their clothes and women wear small bows of white cotton cloth in their hair or pinned to their clothes.

Geomancy, *P'ungsu*

In Korea, geomancy, or *p'ungsu* as it is called, is a method of divining propitious sites for graves, and sometimes houses, buildings, cities and the like. Special care is taken in finding grave sites because a grave orientated with good *p'ungsu* is believed to benefit from the earth's energy and thus exert a lasting and decisive influence over the destinies of the entire family. If a person or a family experiences one misfortune after another, it may be attributed to the disadvantageous location of the home or ancestral tomb and a geomancer may be consulted to find a new location.

The basic theory of *p'ungsu* stems from the belief that the earth is the producer, or mother, of all things. The energy or fever of the earth that is present in each site is believed to exert a powerful influence over those who utilize the land. The inner energy or fever is believed to spring out and the outer energy to ferment, thereby producing wind and water, *p'ung* and *su,* where heaven and earth, which are male and female, are in concord and communicate with each other. The points where the energy is stored and flows are considered propitious sites, or *myŏngdang* in Korean. To find these places involves the use of *yin* and *yang,* the negative and the positive, the two primary principles in nature, and the Five Elements (*ohaeng*), fire, water, wood, metal, and earth.

The most ideal site has a high, rugged mountain to the north, rolling hills to the left and to the right, a low hill to the south, and commands a view of a relatively wide plain through which a river or stream flows. The capital city of Seoul meets these requirements to the letter. The site for the city was chosen by geomancers about six hundred years ago when Yi Sŏng-gye (*see* entry in Historic Figures), the founder of Chosŏn, wished to move the capital of his kingdom. The kingdom and the dynasty which ruled it flourished for over five hundred years.

Marriage, *Kyŏlhon*

In ancient Korea, love and affection had nothing to do with choosing a spouse. In fact, there was very little chance for love to develop as males and females were strictly segregated from the age of seven. Marriages were usually arranged by the parents through a go-between, usually a woman who knew the families well, or a matchmaker, with the aid of a fortuneteller and the couple generally did not meet until the wedding ceremony.

Nowadays there are two paths leading to marriage: *yŏnae* and *chungmae. Yŏnae,* or love match, involves meeting, courting and falling in love. *Chungmae,* or arranged match, involves the arranged meeting of two people through a go-between or match-maker and, upon agreement of the two parties, marriage. Usually, the mothers of the two people and the person responsible for the meeting, the go-between or matchmaker, are present when the two meet. If everyone agrees, the two may be left alone to chat. The prospective couple may date a few times before the wedding but in some cases they do not meet again until the engagement ceremony.

A fortuneteller (*see* Fortunetelling in this chapter) is always consulted in the *chungmae* process. However, it is not uncommon for parents to consult a fortuneteller before giving their consent to a *yŏnae* marriage.

The fortuneteller first examines the *saju,* or four pillars, of the prospective spouse. These are the year, month, day and hour of one's birth as determined by the lunar calendar. These foretell one's fortune; for example, whether one will be successful, rich or poor, or have a long life. However, it is not as simple as it sounds. The *saju p'alcha* (one's *saju* and four pairs of cyclical characters associated with it), are used in a series of complicated calculations to obtain reference numbers to use to consult a fortunetelling book.

If the *saju p'alcha* is satisfactory, the fortuneteller will be asked to divine the *kunghap,* that is, to determine if the man and woman are a harmonious match. This also involves complicated calculations to analyze and compare birth hours.

If the *saju p'alcha* and *kunghap* are acceptable, an engagement ceremony (*yakhŏnshik*) follows with the two families getting together at the woman's house or at a banquet hall but never at the man's house. A piece of white, handmade paper bearing the man's *saju* are presented to the woman's family and the man and woman exchange gifts, usually a watch, a ring or a necklace for the woman and a watch for the man. A discussion usually follows to decide the date for the wedding; a fortuneteller is often consulted prior to the engagement ceremony in order to have several auspicious dates from which to choose.

It is customary for the man's family to send a box containing bridal gifts to the woman's family a few days before the wedding.

The *ham*, as the box is called, is usually delivered at night by friends of the bridegroom. On approaching the house, the bearer of the box calls loudly, *"Ham saseyo!"*, meaning "Box for sale!" The bride's father is expected to come outside to offer money for the box. The buying and selling of the box is usually done with much joking and frolicking. Upon receiving the money, the bearer presents the box to the father and he and his friends are admitted into the house and treated to a feast. During the feast, the father opens the box and examines the contents, usually jewelry and bolts of red and blue silk for a traditional dress. After the feast, the men continue their partying with the money they received for the *ham*.

For traditional weddings, which had long given way to Western-style nuptials but are now gaining in popularity, the groom wears the costume of an ancient court official complete with stiff embroidered belt and horsehair hat and the bride, with red evil-repelling spots painted on her cheeks and forehead, wears the costume of an ancient lady of the court complete with bejewelled coronet. The ceremony, which is usually held outdoors, begins with the groom presenting a goose, usually made of wood, to the bride's parents to indicate that, like the goose, he will be forever faithful to his mate. The groom then takes his place at the east of a high table laden with fruits, candles, red and blue threads, and a goose, duck, or chicken, and the bride, holding a long white cloth in front of her face, is led by two attendants to her place at the west of the table. Then follows a ceremonial hand washing by each and an exchange of bows. They exchange cups of wine and bow to each other again. They then turn and bow to the guests, at which time the bride lowers the cloth from her face. The wedding is completed and the guests can begin feasting.

Western-style weddings are sometimes held in churches but most often in wedding halls, multi-story buildings with numerous weddings going on simultaneously in chambers which vary in size. The groom wears a tailored suit or rented tuxedo and the bride wears a rented wedding gown. The wedding begins with the entrance of the groom and then the bride. The *churye*, usually a highly respected teacher, a government official, a prominent businessman, or a minister, then takes his place as master of ceremonies at a lectern in front of the couple. The *churye* makes a few announcements, gives a speech, tells the bride and groom to greet each other, and proclaims them married. The couple then bow to the guests and walk down the aisle. The wedding is complete, the guests leave for the banquet hall while the newlyweds, wedding participants, families and friends pose for pictures.

The wedding ceremony, whether traditional or Western-style, is followed by another ceremony called *p'yebaek*. For this ceremony, the groom's parents are seated before a table of cooked chicken, jujubes, chestnuts and fruit. The bride and groom bow to them and offer them cups of wine. Then the parents bless the couple by tossing jujubes into their laps as a wish that they bear many children. The bride then bows to other members of the groom's family.

Rites for Confucius, *Sŏkchŏn*

The rites performed to Confucius at the Munmyo shrine (Temple of Confucius; *see* entry in Famous Places and Monuments) are collectively known as *sŏkchŏn*. Meaning "to dispense libations," *sŏkchŏn* refers to the offering of food and drink before the images, portraits or spirit tablets of Confucius and the other sages in the shrine. The rites, which are no longer performed in China where they originated, have been performed at the Munmyo shrine twice a year, in spring and autumn, since 1398.

The basic idea behind the *sŏkchŏn* ritual is that the participants reaffirm the principles of moral management of personal, familial and state affairs and emulate filial piety, virtue, loyalty, honor, social harmony and faith. In other words, it is to foster the ideological and spiritual values of Confucianism.

Throughout the colorful rites the chief officiant can be heard addressing the spirits and cueing the orchestra and dancers. When he finishes there is a prayer and then the other participants in turn offer wine. The same order is repeated for the food offerings.

In ancient times the rites started in the wee hours of the morning with drumming and other musical performances and a great pageant gradually unfolded in prescribed stages. Incense was burned, wine and food offerings were made, stately dances were performed, and invocations and addresses, interspersed with classical court music, were rendered. Following the rites, after all the dignitaries had left the scene, the royal household and the resident scholars of the national Confucian academy (*see* Sŏnggyun-gwan in Famous Places and Monuments) shared the food that had been offered to the sages.

Though the scholars of the Sŏnggyun-gwan always took part in the *sŏkchŏn* rites, the students of today's Sung Kyun Kwan University, which descended from the ancient academy, do not. The Sŏnggyun-gwan Foundation, a private Confucian society, officiates over the much abbreviated rites. The music is performed by the musicians of the National Classical Music Institute and the dances are performed by the students of the National Traditional Music High School. (*see* Confucian Dance, and Confucian Shrine Music in Music and Dance)

Rites for Household Gods, *Kosa*

Kosa refers to the simple shamanistic rituals that are performed to secure the good offices of the household gods. The household gods are discrete for each household and reside everywhere inside and outside the house including its structure. For example, there is the Door Guard (Sumunjang) in the threshold of the gate; the Foundation God (Chishin); the House Lord (Sŏngju) in the roof beam; the Birth Grandmother (Samshin Halmŏni) in the inner room (housewife's room); the Toilet Maid (Pyŏnso Kakssi); the Kitchen God (Chowang); the Mountain God (Sanshin) and the Seven Stars Spirit (Ch'ilsŏng, the Big Dipper) on the terrace where crocks of foodstuffs are stored; and the Five Direction Forces (Obang Shinjang) in every room and stall or pen within the walls.

Depending on the occasion and circumstances, the housewife may make an offering as simple as a cup of water placed beside a burning candle on the lid of a crock or a cup of rice wine and red bean rice cakes or as lavish as a whole pig or cow's head. The House Lord, the House Site Official and the Birth Grandmother are usually given larger piles of rice cakes and more of the more lavish foods because they are considered to be extra special.

Once the housewife has put the offerings in place, she rubs her hands in prayerful supplication, bows and voices her request, usually to make the family rich, the home peaceful and the children turn out well. She leaves the offerings out for a time, perhaps half an hour, and then cuts up the rice cakes, and other foods if the offering has been lavish, and serves them to her family and distributes them to neighbors.

The housewife offers *kosa* after a bountiful harvest or when a significant financial transaction has been made for it is believed that the household gods will become angry and stir up trouble if the wealth is not shared with them. She may do it when her husband is promoted or gets a pay raise or a bonus. If the family moves to another house, the housewife will do *kosa* to bid farewell to the gods so that they will not follow the family to their new home and cause trouble and she will do it in the new house to ensure that the family will receive blessings from the gods of that house.

When a child is born, *kosa* of rice and seaweed soup must be offered for seven days to the Birth Grandmother, the god of the inner room who oversees conception, gestation, birth and lactation. Special offerings must also be made to her on the fourteenth, twenty-first and hundredth day after birth and on the first birthday so that she will not feel neglected and will continue to protect the baby from harm. *Kosa* may also be done for her when a woman is barren in the hope that she will grant conception.

Kosa is also done when there is a death in the house because the changes it causes in family relationships confuses the gods so they must be honored lest they become frustrated and flee, leaving the house unprotected. A sickness in the family is also cause for *kosa* because it could be due to an unhappy god.

There are also certain days that *kosa* are traditionally performed. These include days of great feasting such as Sŏl (Lunar New Year's) and Ch'usŏk (Harvest Moon) because the gods like to feast too. Tano, the fifth day of the fifth lunar month when farmers traditionally enjoy a day of rest with various forms of competition, is a time to treat the gods to the summer foods that are coming into season. Ch'ilsŏk, the seventh day of the seventh lunar month, when the rice planting is usually completed, is a time to honor the gods in the hope that they will watch over the fields and thereby ensure a good harvest.

Kosa is performed many times during the first lunar month and especially on the full moon. It is performed often at this time to ask that the new year be filled with good luck and prosperity, protection from bad spirits, a good harvest, health, happiness and the like.

Kosa may be performed for the opening of a new building, the moving of an office, the completion of building repairs and the like. Such *kosa* are officiated by men and performed mainly for the House Site Official (T'ŏju Taegam), the god who governs the total area within the walls of the structure and thus influences the prosperity and good fortune of those within.

Rites for Royalty, *Chehyang*

The Confucian rites performed at the Chongmyo shrine (*see* entry in Famous Places and Monuments) to honor the spirits of the twenty-seven Yi Dynasty kings and their queens are collectively known as *chehyang*. During the Chosŏn period (1392-1910), the rites were held five times a year for the kings who had direct heirs to the throne and twice a year for the kings who had no direct heirs or who were posthumously honored with the title of king. The rites were abolished in the early part of the twentieth century but were resumed in 1969, though in the form of one large service held annually. The service is held every first Sunday in May by the Yi Dynasty Association which consists of descendants of the royal Yi family.

In the past the rites were performed by the king, civil and military court officials, and other lesser nobles. At that time, the day began with the king selecting the food offerings from choice cows, goats and pigs and the finest fruits, grains and honey brought to the capital from the provinces.

Although the food selection is done differently, the rites are still performed in much the same manner they were in the past. To the accompaniment of stately music, praising either the civil achievements of the king or his military exploits and achievements, the participants offer wine in brass cups to the spirits of the kings and queens. The food offerings are on tables before the spirit tablets *(wip'ae)* in the cubicles of the shrine. (*see* Royal Ancestral Shrine Music in Music and Dance)

Sebae, New Year's Obeisance

A traditional New Year's custom is to pay respect to one's elders by giving a deep bow. Called *sebae,* this type of obeisance is made to family members who are older or of an older generation and may be made to elderly neighbors as well.

It is customary for those who receive *sebae* to reciprocate in some way. Children are usually given money *(ton),* at which time it is referred to as "*sebaetton,*" and told to study hard, to obey their parents, or some other appropriate remarks. Adults are usually given well-wishing remarks appropriate to their situation, such as "I'm sure you will be blessed with a son this year," or "I'm sure you will be promoted this year," and served food and drink.

Shamanism, Musok

Shamanism (Musok), the belief that every object in the natural world has a spirit, is Korea's most ancient indigenous tradition. It is believed to have entered Korea with Altaic migrants from the north deep in Korea's prehistoric past.

It was the leading religion and the core of political and social ideologies during the ancient tribal kingdoms down to the Three Kingdoms period (1st century B.C.–7th century A.D.). It began to decline with the establishment of Buddhism as the state religion and ideological guide of the Unified Shilla Kingdom (668-935) and it was severely ostracized during the highly Confucian Chosŏn Kingdom (1392-1910). Throughout its long history, it incorporated many elements from Buddhism, Taoism and Confucianism while at the same time exerting a tremendous influence on the three.

Korean Shamanism attributes spirits, which affect the lives of the living, to human beings as well as to all natural forces and inanimate objects such as wind, rain, mountains, rocks and trees. Over all of the spirits rules Hanŭnim, Lord of Heaven, the Celestial Emperor of the Heavenly Kingdom. After death, good people are believed to become good spirits and reside in the Heavenly Kingdom and bad people are believed to become evil spirits and reside in the Kingdom of Darkness or the Underworld that is both subterranean and subaquatic. Goblins are believed to be the spirits of good people who have died but for some reason have not been permitted to enter the world of the blessed and so wander through the world of the living. Ghosts, on the other hand, are believed to be the spirits of unhappy or wicked people who have been refused entrance into the other worlds and are awaiting their release from the world of the living.

The shaman, or *manshin* (vulgarly called *mudang*), now usually a woman, mediates between this world and the spiritual world to dissolve conflicts and tensions that are believed to exist between the dead and the living by reconciling the two. These conflicts and tensions are believed to be the cause of various diseases and misfortune. She also communicates with the spiritual world to ask protection, blessings, etc. for those of the living.

To communicate with the spirit world, the *manshin* must enlist the help of a large pantheon of nature spirits, Taoist deities, reincarnated Buddhist deities, and ancestor spirits. She must enter a state of trance, undergoing, in the process, psychological stress and a transformation of character as she becomes possessed by spirits. This she does through a ritual called *kut* which involves offerings, music, dance, drama, acrobatics and theatrics. She invokes the presence of spirits, receives oracles from them, entertains them and sends them back from whence they came.

Manshin perform innumerable rites. For example, rites are performed for a good harvest, for safety at sea, for good fishing, for childbirth, for curing disease, and for repelling evil. They are also performed to honor the Mountain Spirit (Sanshin), the Seven Star Spirit (Ch'ilsŏng, the Big Dipper), the Birth Grandmother (Samshin Halmŏni), the Heavenly God (Ch'ŏnshin), the Dragon God (Yongshin), the General God (Changgunshin), and the King God (Wangshin), which are the major deities, as well as numerous household and village gods.

There are also shamanic rituals that are performed by people other than *manshin*. For example, there are rites, called *kosa* (*see* Rites for Household Gods in this chapter), that are made when one moves into a new house, launches a boat, opens a new office and the like. There are also rites that are made to the Birth Grandmother at the time of childbirth, one hundred days after birth and on the first birthday. There are also rites to honor village tutelary deities that are said to reside in large trees (*tang namu* or *sŏnangdang*) and in *changsŭng* (*see* entry in this chapter), man-shaped spirit posts that guard the entrances to villages and temples. The term *sŏnangdang* is used for a variety of shrines for a variety of tutelary deities.

Taejonggyo

Taejonggyo is an indigenous Korean religion embodying a national myth. The central concept of the four thousand-year-old religion is a triune god called Hanul who embodies creator, teacher and temporal king. Hanul took human form in the person of Tan-gun (*see* entry in Historic Figures), the father, teacher and king of the Korean people who supposedly descended from heaven in 2333 B.C.

Tan-gun established rituals for offering prayers of praise and propitiation to heaven and by the end of the Three Kingdoms period they were strongly established among nobles and commoners alike. However, purity in the practice of Taejonggyo gradually declined with the introduction of foreign religions and by the fifteenth century it had practically disappeared. A resurgence of nationalism in the late nineteenth century as well as in more recent years has led to the emergence of a number of sects claiming to be a revival of Taejonggyo.

Talismans, *Pujŏk*

Talismans, or *pujŏk* as they are called in Korean, are used by Koreans to protect against evil spirits that cause sickness, bad luck and various forms of calamity by enlisting the aid of well-intended spirits. They are believed to be able to influence human actions and feelings as well as individual fate.

The usual practice is to have a *pujŏk* prepared by a qualified fortuneteller, monk or shaman. A red ink, ideally cinnabar, is used to draw the talismanic formula onto a sheet of yellow mulberry paper. Red, according to traditional color symbolism, has the power to suppress evil and yellow is believed to go well with red, artistically and metaphysically. The formula may be represented by a single Chinese character, or a line of Sanskrit, or a line of Chinese incorporated in a labyrinth of religious symbols, star charts, birds, animals and other figures. Stylistically they range from free-form swirls and doodles to highly geometric patterns.

Depending on the goal for which it was made, the *pujŏk* may be attached to a wall, put under one's pillow, buried, carried in one's pocket, sewn in one's clothing, or ingested after being burnt and the ashes mixed with tea or water. Traditionally, New Year's and the onset of spring (Ipch'un) are times for posting *pujŏk* in places in and around the house such as on the gate, over the door, on the ceiling beam and in the storage room.

Pujŏk are benign by nature; they are used to correct or prevent a problem, not to cause one. Some common uses of them are: to ward off or drive out disease, to secure a good job, to insure safe travel, to insure marital bliss, to get rid of a spouse's lover, to give birth to a male child, to enjoy a long life, to protect against thieves, to do a flourishing business, and to dream a happy dream.

Taoism, Togyo

Taoism, or Togyo as it is called in Korean, was introduced to Korea in the seventh century A.D. when a Taoist monk took

Taoist texts and statues of Taoist divinities to Koguryŏ. With time it came to permeate all strata of the Korean populace because its syncretic worship of a multiplicity of gods readily fit in with Korea's animistic beliefs and because it freely borrowed from Confucianism and Buddhism in its institutions, temples, ceremonies and canon. However, it failed to deeply affect government and the general society because of its philosophy that development of civilization is a degradation of the natural order and its ideal of a return to original purity.

The most apparent trace of Taoist influence in Korea is the search for longevity and good fortune which is manifest in the symbols, both auspicious and protective, which abound in Korean art, especially in the decorative arts. *Shipchangsaeng* (*see* entry in Arts and Crafts), ten animals and objects symbolizing long life, is one of the most frequently encountered motifs. The ten animals and objects are rocks, mountains, water, clouds, pine trees, the Fungus of Immortality (*pulloch'o*), tortoises, deer, cranes and the sun. One of the most conspicuous uses of Taoist symbols is in the Korean flag (*see* entry in Miscellaneous).

Zodiac, *Shibiji*

The Oriental zodiac, which is used not only in Korea but throughout Asia, is called *shibiji* in Korean. It has a twelve-year cycle. Each year is named for a different animal who imparts its own distinct characteristics to that year and to those born within it. Thus the traditional way to ask a person's age in Korea is to ask his or her zodiacal animal, or *tti* in Korean. The twelve zodiacal animals are also used to name the twelve two-hour periods into which the day is divided and impart their characteristics to each period and to those born in that period. This is very important in fortunetelling (*see* entry in this chapter), especially in determining a suitable time for weddings, funerals and other major events in one's life.

The twelve animals are the symbols of the Twelve Terrestrial Branches, which is part of the cycle of sixty that is the basis of the lunar calendar (*see* entry in Lifestyle). Though the lunar calendar was developed in China, supposedly in 2637 B.C. by the legendary Emperor Huang-Ti, some scholars believe the twelve animals were borrowed from the Turks. Needless to say, the Oriental zodiac has been in use since around the time of Christ.

The animals of the zodiac and the characteristics of those born under them are:

Rat: timid, humble, energetic, ambitious, quick to anger, stingy, perseverant, and gossipy.

Ox: strong, steady, patient, hard working, dextrous, quiet, placid, easygoing, stubborn, success oriented, and eccentric.

Tiger: sensitive, stubborn, short-tempered, speculative, sympathetic, courageous, headstrong, prone to selfishness and a bit mean and obstinate.

Rabbit: good-natured, placid, affectionate, friendly, melancholic, reserved, virtuous, talented, and complacent.

Dragon: quick, excitable, short-tempered, stubborn, energetic, honest, sensitive, brave and trust inspiring.

Snake: intelligent, attractive, quiet, pensive, vain, passionate, determined, and somewhat crafty and antagonistic.

Horse: quick, impatient, hot-blooded, quick to anger, independent, and perceptive.

Sheep: artistic, tender, kind, timid, generous, sympathetic, and unassertive.

Monkey: passionate, strong-willed, clever, skillful, financially adroit, and contemptuous.

Cock: pensive, ambitious but without foresight, brave, outspoken and often improvident.

Dog: honest, loyal, confidence-inspiring, eccentric, cold emotionally, and can be selfish, stubborn and critical.

Boar: honest, chivalrous, gallant, affectionate, kind, studious, short-tempered and impulsive.

LIFESTYLE

Dress

The Korean costume is called *hanbok*. It is characterized by simple lines and no pockets. The women's *hanbok* comprises a wrap skirt and a bolero-like jacket, and the men's, roomy pants bound at the ankles and a short jacket. *Hanbok* are worn by Koreans of all ages, particularly on traditional holidays and when attending social affairs having a Korean overtone.

Some of the basic elements of today's *hanbok*, namely the jacket *(chŏgori)* and pants *(paji)*, were probably worn at a very early date, but it was not until the Three Kingdoms period (57 B.C.-A.D. 668) that the two-piece costume of today began to evolve. Short, tight trousers and tight, waist-length jackets were worn by both men and women during the early part of the period as evidenced by ancient tomb paintings.

Toward the end of the Three Kingdoms period, T'ang China introduced Koreans to silk mandarin robes and they were adopted for wear by royalty and officials. Noblewomen began to wear full-length skirt-trousers and wide-sleeved, hip-length jackets belted at the waist and noblemen began to wear roomy trousers bound in at the ankles and a narrow, tunic-style jacket cuffed at the wrists and belted at the waist.

In the late thirteenth century Koryŏ, the kingdom that ruled Korea from 918-1392, became a vassal state of Mongolia during the Mongol Chinese Yuan Dynasty. Its twenty-fifth ruler, Ch'ungnyŏl-wang (r. 1274-1308), took as his wife a princess from the court of Kubla Khan and began dressing in Mongol fashion. It is said that within three years of his ascendance to the throne, every official in the Koryŏ court had shaved his head except for a patch of hair in the middle and had adopted the dress of the Mongolian plains people. During the short time Koryŏ was a Mongol vassal, three kings were born to Korean-Mongolian queens, which had quite an effect on the social and fashion trends of the times. The skirt (ch'ima) was shortened as was the vest (chŏgori), which was hiked up above the waist and tied at the chest with a long, wide ribbon instead of belted and the sleeves were curved slightly.

Women of Chosŏn, the kingdom that superseded Koryŏ in 1392 and was ruled by the highly Confucian Yi Dynasty, began to wear pleated skirts and longer vests in the fifteenth century. Upper-class women wore full-length skirts to indicate their social standing. The vest was gradually shortened until it just covered the breasts. This made it necessary to reduce the fullness of the skirt somewhat so that it could be extended almost to the armpits, which remains the fashion.

The upper classes wore *hanbok* of closely woven ramie cloth or other high-grade lightweight materials in warm weather and of plain and patterned silks the rest of the year. Commoners were restricted by law as well as resources to cotton at best. The upper classes wore a variety of colors, though bright colors were generally worn by children and young girls and subdued colors by middle-aged men and women. Commoners were restricted by law to everyday clothes of white but for special occasions they wore dull shades of pale pink, light green, grey and charcoal.

Both males and females wore their hair in a long pigtail until they were married, at which time the hair was knotted—the man's in a topknot (sangt'u) on the top of the head and the woman's in a ball just above the nape of the neck. A long pin, or *pinyŏ*, was thrust through the knotted hair of the woman as both a fastener and a decoration. The material and length of the *pinyŏ* varied according to the wearer's class and status. Headwear for men varied according to class and status.

Family System

In Korea the community has always centered around the extended family, comprising parents, their sons and their wives and children and often other relatives. In the old days, the typical family was very large with often several generations living together.

Traditionally, the first son *(changja)* continued to live at home, even after marriage, to care for his parents the rest of their lives. He inherited the family property and was in charge of the all-important ancestral rites (*see* entry in Beliefs and Customs). Younger sons also continued to live at home after marriage, but only temporarily; the length varied according to the family's particular circumstances and the region. Younger sons eventually established their own households, referred to by other family members as *chagŭnjip*, meaning "little house" or "minor house." The oldest son's household was called *k'ŭnjip*, meaning "big house."

A daughter, unlike a son, left her natal household to become part of her husband's natal household. Thus, the phrase *shijip kada*, literally meaning "go to in-laws' house," is used to refer to a woman getting married. And, of course, depending on her husband's line of descent, she would live in the *k'ŭnjip* or in a separate household. Her social transition from her natal household and kin group to her husband's was a lifelong process and she was a marginal member of both kin groups, her marriage having made her an outsider to her own natal family. The birth of her first child strengthened her ties with her husband's family, especially if it was a male because it would ensure the family's continuity for another generation. At the same time, a male would ensure that she would be venerated after death.

Husband and wife refer to each other, respectively, as *pakkat saram* or *pakkat yangban*, meaning "outside person," and *an saram* meaning "one inside." The woman's place was in the home, taking care of the household, whereas the man's was outside.

The head of the family was regarded as the source of authority, and all members were expected to obey and respect him. It was unthinkable for children or grandchildren to oppose or go against the wishes of their parents or grandparents or betray their expectations. On the other hand, it was expected that the head of the family would be fair in dealing with the family members. Order at home was maintained through obedience and deference to superiors, that is, children obeying parents, the wife the husband, the younger siblings the older, and so forth, which has its roots in filial piety, the greatest of all Confucian virtues.

While the large extended family is rapidly becoming a thing of the past, the roles and relations within the family remain largely unchanged.

Food

Korean cuisine ranges in taste from bland to peppery hot and includes a wide variety of wild and cultivated vegetables and animals, many that are eaten for their aromatic and medicinal properties. Most foods are prepared by stir-frying, steaming, braising, grilling, poaching, boiling or barbecuing and most carry the blended tang and aroma of garlic, red pepper, green onions, soy sauce, and sesame seeds and oil.

Rice (*pap*), either plain or cooked with other grains such as barley and millet and/or a variety of beans, is the main dish. *Kimch'i*, a pungent, fermented dish generally comprising cabbage or turnip seasoned with salt, garlic, leeks, ginger, red pepper and shellfish, is the next most important component of a Korean meal.

Soup (*kuk*) is also a vital part of every meal. Spicy or bland, it generally contains meat, fish, or seaweed. Thick soups made of soybean paste (*toenjang*) and soybean curd are especially popular. Rounding out the meal are what are called *panch'an,* or side dishes. These generally include a seafood or meat dish and parboiled vegetables, herbs and roots that are lightly seasoned with sesame oil, garlic, soy sauce and ground and toasted sesame seeds.

Kimch'i is Korea's most famous food. It spikes the rice, titillates the tastebuds, and supplies many vitamins and minerals. There are basically two kinds of *kimch'i,* seasonal and winter, with numerous varieties of each. The seasonal varieties are made with whatever vegetables are available and are eaten right away or within a few days. However, the winter varieties are made with mostly cabbages and turnips and are stored away to be eaten during the cold winter months when fresh vegetables are scarce. The *kimjang kimch'i,* as the winter variety is called, is usually stored in crockery jars. The storage temperature should be well controlled to prevent over fermentation and thus souring. The traditional way of doing this is to bury the crocks in the ground.

There are a number of holiday foods and special dishes that are a must for important celebrations. These include *ttŏk,* rice cakes dusted with roasted soy or embellished with aromatic mugwort leaves, and *ttŏkkuk,* a rice-dumpling soup that is a must on New Year's Day.

Dishes called *anju* always accompany liquor *(sul).* These generally consist of meat, seafood, or dried fish, nuts, and fruit.

Meals are usually eaten at low tables on the floor. The *kimch'i, panch'an* and main dishes are placed in the middle of the table to be shared by everyone. Each person has his own bowl of rice and soup. Eating is done with a long-handled spoon *(sutkarak)* and a pair of chopsticks *(chŏtkarak)* which are collectively called *sujŏ.*

Housing

Korean houses tradition-ally consisted of a court-yard surrounded by high walls and one-story buildings comprising several rooms and halls. The buildings were gen-erally arranged around the courtyard to form a

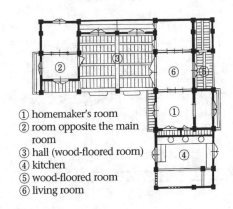

① homemaker's room
② room opposite the main room
③ hall (wood-floored room)
④ kitchen
⑤ wood-floored room
⑥ living room

ㄱ, ㄷ, or ㅁ shape. Of course, a large or wealthy upper-class family would have any number of courtyards and buildings and there would be a women's quarters *(anch'ae)*, a men's quarters *(sarangch'ae)*, a servants quarters *(haengnangch'ae)*, and an ancestral shrine *(sadang)* containing memorial tablets.

The buildings were elevated and had wood and clay walls and tiled roofs. The corners of the roofs tilted slightly upward giving the buildings a smiling appearance. On the outside of the buildings were long narrow verandahs with polished wood floors where one would sit to remove one's shoes before entering a room through a latticed door covered with paper. The verandahs *(t'oetmaru)* were on the same level as the interior floors.

The main rooms in which the family lived had floors made of stone and baked clay covered with oiled paper. They were heated by a Korean method called *ondol,* a system using under-the-floor flues to carry warm air from a central source of heat such as a kitchen fire or outside fire. The rooms were generally small with low ceilings to make the most of the heating system. The halls, which not only connected the rooms but also served as extra living space in warm weather, had polished wooden floors called *maru.* The family sat on mats or cushions on the floor and slept on mats on the floor which were rolled up and stored away during the day. The rooms were furnished with low tables and various chests and cupboards.

Male and female members of the extended family led largely separated lives in keeping with the Confucian dictate, "At the age of seven, boys and girls shall cease to sit side by side." Sexual

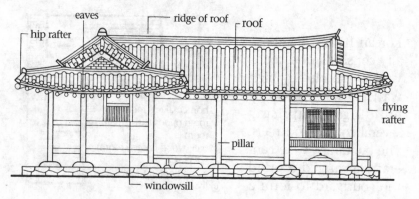

segregation was most strictly adhered to in *yangban*, or upper class, households. The men spent their days in rooms near the main gate and the women in rooms at the rear of the house.

The main room of the men's quarters was the *sarangbang*, where the master of the house studied and received guests. It usually had a spacious verandah-like elevated wooden floor with wooden railings called *numaru* that commanded a good view of a garden. The *sarangbang* was usually furnished with low stationery chests, book shelves, a writing table, an inkstone table, a tea table, a document chest, one or two letter racks, a smoking tray, and several flower vases and lamp stands. The furniture was functional and characterized by simple lines, restrained ornamentation and subdued colors. It was meant to be practical and conducive to scholarly pursuits.

The main room of the women's quarters was the *anbang*. It was the center of the home and the rest of the house was positioned around it. It was where the mistress of the house slept at night and from where she ran the household during the day. It was usually furnished with various chests and boxes. These included two- and three-story clothing chests called *ich'ŭngjang* and *samch'ŭngjang* and pairs of stacking chests called *nong*. *Mŏrijang*, low, one-story chests for storing valuables, were placed where the head of the sleeping mat would be when spread out on the floor at night. The chests were generally colorful and elaborately decorated. Cosmetic boxes with folding mirrors called *kyŏngdae*, comb boxes and sewing boxes were also essential furnishings of the *anbang*.

The *anbang* was connected to the other rooms by a spacious wooden-floored hall called *taech'ŏng* that was, in effect, a pantry. Its walls were lined with massive chests for storing rice, food shelves and cupboards *(twiju, ch'antak,* and *ch'anjang)*. It was the main place for family gatherings, especially rituals and ceremonies.

There was no dining room in traditional Korean homes. Meals were carried from the kitchen *(puŏk)*, which was located near the *anbang* or connected to it, to the various rooms on a combination serving and dining table called *sang* or *soban*. In a sunny place in the yard, not far from the kitchen, was the sauce jar terrace, or *changdoktae.* This was where soy sauce, bean paste, red pepper paste and other foodstuff was stored in crockery jars.

Country houses, especially farm houses, usually had thatched roofs. They also had storage facilities and cattle sheds within the walls of the housing compound.

Deep in the mountains, houses were often made of logs and roofed with pine or fir bark. This type of house, called *nŏwajip,* was not enclosed behind walls or fences.

Thatched houses, called *ch'ogajip,* are now rarely seen. But houses with tiled roofs, called *hanok,* are still a common sight in some areas.

Lunar Calendar

The Gregorian calendar, or *yangnyŏk,* meaning "solar calendar," has been the official calendar of Korea since it was adopted by the government in 1895. However, the lunar calendar, or *ŭmnyŏk,* which has been used throughout the Orient for centuries, is used for reckoning the dates of traditional festivals and many people celebrate their birthday by it. It is said to have been developed in China in 2637 B.C. by the legendary Emperor Huang-ti.

This old calendar is called the lunar calendar because each new month begins with the new moon. However, it is also solar in that the year is divided into twenty-four solar terms or periods and it is adjusted to the timing of the seasons. The twenty-four solar terms correspond to the day on which the sun enters the first and fifteenth degree of the twelve zodiacal signs, and thus are approximately fifteen days long.

The first day in each month is the new moon, and the fifteenth day is the full moon. Some months have thirty days and some twenty-nine. As the twelve months do not equal a solar year, an extra month, called *yundal* in Korean, is interposed every three years. The extra month is interposed between any two months from the second to the eleventh in a way that only one of the twenty-four solar terms will fall in the intercalary month;

however, the vernal equinox must fall in the second month, the summer solstice in the fifth month, the autumn equinox in the eighth month, and the winter solstice in the eleventh month.

Each year is named according to the combination of two sets of Chinese characters. One set, the Celestial Stems *(shipkan)* has ten basic characters and the other set, the Terrestrial Branches *(shibiji)*, has twelve, which are symbolized by the twelve animals of the zodiac *(see* entry in Beliefs and Customs). As the least common multiple of ten and twelve is sixty, the cycle of combinations recommences every sixty years, which is why the sixtieth birthday, or *hwan-gap (see* Birthdays in Beliefs and Customs), is considered a major milestone in one's life.

The traditional way to ask a person's age is to ask his or her zodiacal animal, or *tti* in Korean. The twelve animals are also used to divide the day into twelve two-hour periods.

The days of the week are named for the sun, the moon, and the planets Mars, Mercury, Jupiter, Venus and Saturn. The ancient Chinese named the planets for the Five Elements *(ohaeng)*–fire, water, wood, metal and earth–and it is by these names they are known today. The naming of the days in this way was originally done to facilitate divination, which otherwise required costly, and often unavailable, books and charts giving the daily positions of heavenly bodies to determine the actual position of the moon.

Names

A Korean name, or *irŭm,* is usually made up of three Chinese characters, each character pronounced as a single syllable. The surname *(sŏng)* is placed first. The given name is usually made up of two characters, one of which is chosen by the clan and is used by all members of the same generation. This character, or generation marker, is called *tollimja* or *hangnyŏl.* It usually, but not always, alternates between the second and third place in the name, and changes from one generation to the next according to a complex cycle involving the Chinese theory of the Five Elements (*ohaeng*) fire, water, wood, metal, and earth. Some families give generation markers to female offspring, but most do not since by tradition females are excluded from performing ancestral rites and since their names are not usually recorded in the family *chokpo*, the genealogical table that traces one's lineage back to the progenitor of one's clan.

There is a great variety of given names but a limited number of surnames. There are two hundred seventy-four surnames in current use but forty-four of them account for less than one hundred persons each. Kim, Lee (Yi) and Park (Pak) are the surnames of approximately 45 percent of the total Korean population. While most surnames are of one character, there are some two-character surnames. And, while most given names are of two characters, there are some of one character and some of three characters. Of course, each character of a Korean name has a certain meaning, but that is a story in itself which could fill many tomes.

According to traditional belief, a child's fate is influenced by the name it is given so it is not uncommon for the parents, or the paternal grandfather who is usually given the honor of naming the child, to consult a professional name maker, or *changmyŏngga*. The name maker can choose a character which can combine perfectly with the surname and the generation marker to form a name that will ensure success for the child which will in turn bring honor to the family. And, as one might guess, it is not uncommon for a person to change his or her name when it is thought to be the root of some misfortune or other trouble. Of course, this also requires consultation with a name maker.

The origin of Korean surnames is somewhat hazy. Most apparently derived from Chinese family names which were used sometime during the early years of the Three Kingdoms period (1st century B.C.-7th century A.D.). Originally having no surnames, early Koreans appear to have taken Chinese family names when they came under the influence of Chinese culture.

Given names are seldom used except in the family, between classmates, or between very close friends who have agreed to call each other by their given names. Terms of kinship, for example the Korean equivalents of older brother, older sister, uncle, aunt, grandfather and grandmother, are used instead of names when addressing or referring to older people. Even spouses avoid using each other's name; for example, the parents of a child named Sun-hi may refer to each other as Sun-hi's Father or Sun-hi's Mother in conversations with others. Names are not a part of polite social intercourse except when used to refer to someone not present. A person is addressed by his or her title, position, scholastic rank, or by an honorific. Women keep their own surname when they marry. They are usually referred to as their child's mother, for example, Sun-hi's Mother, or by a title in deference to their husband's position, for example, Samonim, meaning "teacher's wife."

Seals, *Tojang*

A seal bearing one's name is more important than one's signature in Korea, especially on legal documents. Called *tojang* in Korean, they are used in all kinds of business transactions by both individuals and organizations. Legal transactions, for example, the purchase of real estate, require the use of a special seal called *in-gam tojang*. This is a seal that is registered with the government so that authenticity can be proven.

Seals may be of any shape but the most common are round, oval and square. Individuals tend to use small ones about one-fourth inch in diameter and one and a half inches long that can be carried easily. Organizations use large ones one or two inches in diameter or square and several inches long. Seals are usually carved of hardwood, ivory, jade, marble, smoky

topaz, and nowadays plastic. The ink for making the impression is made of a sticky scarlet vegetable dye that is permanent.

The use of seals was originally introduced from China during the Three Kingdoms period (1st century B.C.-7th century A.D.). It was a status symbol for royalty and any transfer of power was represented by the handing over of the imperial seals. During the Koryŏ Kingdom (918-1392), seals came to be used by individuals and seal carving developed into an art.

Traditional Medicine, *Hanbang*

Hanbang, meaning "Korean prescription," is a term that has come to be used for a variety of traditional healing techniques. These include herbal medicine *(hanyak)*, acupuncture *(ch'im)*, pressure point massage *(chiap)*, and moxibustion *(ttŭm)*.

These healing techniques were originally introduced from China in the sixth century A.D. They were further developed and assimilated with ancient Korean pharmacology and eventually introduced to Japan.

The theory behind these techniques is that the human body has fourteen physiological systems, each associated with a major visceral organ and a line, or pathway, through which a force called *ki* circulates according to a certain rhythm. Sickness, or disease occurs when the flow of *ki* is disturbed and can occur either in the organ associated with the line in which the disturbance occurred or at a point along the line. The various healing techniques are thus designed to correct imbalances and excesses in or eliminate blockages of the flow of *ki*.

The philosophy behind the theory embodies two major principles of the universe: the *yin-yang* principle of dualism and the principle of the Five Elements *(ohaeng*: fire, water, wood, metal, and earth). According to the *yin-yang* principle, or *um-yang* in Korean, life is controlled by two contrasting forces: the *yin* and the *yang*, the negative and the positive, the dark and the light, the female and the male. If a proper relationship exists between these forces, in medicine the union is called health; an improper relationship or imbalance results in sickness or disease. According to the principle of the Five Elements, or *ohaeng* in Korean, everything in the universe is derived from the five basic elements: water, fire, wood, metal, and earth. The elements are mutually friendly or antagonistic to each other: Water produces wood, but destroys fire; fire produces earth, but destroys metal; metal produces water, but destroys wood; wood produces fire, but destroys earth; and earth produces metal, but destroys water. Through this operation of antagonism and synergism, the Five Elements maintain a state of harmony and equilibrium that, in medicine, is called good health. Thus to treat a sick person, a medical practitioner must help restore the forces of *yin-yang* to their proper balance by repressing or stimulating one or the other force and by returning the Five Elements to a state of harmony.

There are four methods of physical examination: *shijin*, observation of the face and overall appearance of the person; *munjin*, listening to the sound of the person's voice; *munjin*, (the Chinese character is different from the previous *munjin*), questioning the person about his medical history and symptoms; and, *chŏlchin*, palpation of the pulse and stomach. All four methods are employed to insure a correct diagnosis. The pulse reading is very important. It is done by placing three fingers along the radial pulse at the wrist and is felt in each finger separately. There are seventeen types of pulses, each requiring a different treatment.

Once the diagnosis is made, the practitioner may prescribe acupuncture, which involves inserting needles into a number of the three hundred sixty-five insertion points located on the lines of *ki*, an herbal tonic, moxibustion or a combination of them. Treatment almost always involves a change in diet because a person's diet effects the *yin-yang* and the Five Elements. Moreover, food is also classified as being *yin, yang* or neutral in character and thus gives balance and harmony to the body. Too much *yin* food or too much *yang* food can thus weaken the body and lead to sickness.

The tonics are made of herbal, animal and mineral elements according to prescriptions contained in *Tong-ŭi pogam (Exemplar of Korean Medicine)*, a twenty-five volume medical book based on ancient Korean and Chinese treatises on medicine that was published in 1610. Among the most common ingredients for tonics are licorice, mugwort, iris root, deer antler, and ginseng. Dog meat soup *(poshin t'ang)*, snake soup *(paem t'ang)*, and snake wine *(paem sul)* are commonly prescribed health rejuvenators.

Ginseng, which is shaped like a man and thus called *insam*, or man root, in Korean, is considered an elixir of life. It is consumed in many forms. It is eaten raw, made into tea and liquor, taken in capsules, added to foods, and even made into chewing gum. A very popular ginseng dish that is considered a health rejuvenator is *samgye t'ang*, a spring chicken stuffed with ginseng, jujubes, chestnuts, and glutinous rice and cooked several hours in its own broth.

SPECIAL DAYS

Ch'op'ail, Buddha's Birthday

The eighth day of the fourth lunar month is Buddha's birthday. It is called Ch'op'ail, literally meaning "eighth day of the month," and also Puch'ŏnim Oshinnal, literally meaning "the day Buddha came." This day has been a legal holiday in Korea since 1975.

Buddhists celebrate this day with many events and much merrymaking. Among them are a symbolic bathing of the baby Buddha. This is done using a special vessel to pour water over a statue of a baby Buddha which stands in a lotus-shaped basin. This ritual is not limited to monks but can be done by anyone who so desires.

Another ritual in which laymen can participate is called *t'aptori*. A group of Buddhists led by a monk form a ring and circle a *t'ap*, or pagoda, praying and chanting sutras.

The highlight of the day is the lighting of paper lanterns which are hung everywhere inside and outside the temple. Believers hang a lantern for each member of the family. These are usually purchased in advance from the resident monks who hang them and chant prayers for the subscribers throughout the day. The lanterns are lit in the evening.

To the Buddhist, the lantern symbolizes wisdom and mercy. The lanterns are said to brighten and eliminate the dark spots in one's heart as the light is believed to be given by the Buddha.

The lanterns are made of paper or plastic, but in olden times they were made of silk or paper. They come in a variety of shapes including octagonal, lotus flower, phoenix, carp, cloud, drum, and turtle. The most common are octagonal and lotus shaped. In some towns and cities, the lanterns are carried in a parade which may include elaborate floats.

Ch'usŏk, Harvest Moon Festival

The fifteenth day of the eighth lunar month is Ch'usŏk, the Harvest Moon Festival, a time of thanksgiving. Also called Chungch'ujŏl, meaning "mid-autumn day," and Han-gawi, the origin of which is unclear, it is a time for families to get together at the oldest male member's house for a great feast to celebrate the new harvest and, more importantly, to offer thanks and to show respect to Nature and to their ancestors.

Ch'usŏk is believed to have originated in the first century A.D. During the reign of Yuri-wang (r. 24-57) of the Shilla Kingdom, a month-long weaving festival was held in the capital, today's Kyŏngju. For the contest, the king divided the city into two teams and appointed princesses to lead them. The king announced the winner on the day of the eighth full moon and the losing team had to provide food, drink, and entertainment for the winning team and a party involving the whole city ensued.

Regardless of origin, Ch'usŏk and its related customs are undeniably important to Koreans. And when Ch'usŏk dawns, they don their best outfits and, like generations before them, begin a series of rituals and activities culminating in gazing at the full moon.

The first order of the day is to pay homage to the ancestors with a feast of foods made from the new harvest. It is offered in solemn rites called *ch'arye* (*see* Ancestral Rites in Beliefs and Customs). Among the offerings are watery radish *kimch'i* (*see* Food in Lifestyle), meat, fish, chestnuts, persimmons, jujubes, pears, apples, and the specialty of the day, stuffed rice cakes called *songp'yŏn*. The rice cakes, which are shaped like a half moon, are made of dough made of flour milled from newly harvested rice, and steamed on a layer of freshly picked pine needles. The pine needles give the rice cakes a nice fragrance and help preserve them. The fillings vary from region to region but the most common are sesame seeds, chestnuts, beans and jujubes.

On Ch'usŏk, it is customary to visit the graves of one's ancestors to pay respect with bows and food offerings. It is also a time to cut the grass and pull up weeds on and around the grave.

There are a number of games and dances associated with Ch'usŏk, which, in the past, helped to strengthen neighborly relations and to promote community spirit. Among the most notable is *kŏbuk-nori,* the tortoise game. In this game, or *nori,* the *kŏbuk,* or tortoise, is two men on their hands and knees covered with a large shell made of straw or corn leaves. The tortoise is driven like an ox from house to house throughout the village by a group of men to entertain and be entertained in return. The tortoise dances and performs antics for a while and then collapses, pretending to be hungry and exhausted. The householder then treats everyone with food and drink and they all sing and dance together.

Kanggangsuwollae (*see* entry in Music and Dance) is a circle dance performed by women in the southwestern part of Korea. It supposedly developed from a trick women played on Japanese invaders in the sixteenth century by dancing around fires in the evening to make them believe their target was well defended. The lyrics of the song the dancers sing express desires for happiness, longevity and love while describing typical household scenes. The refrain, *kanggangsuwollae,* means "watch or guard the surroundings." However, being traditionally associated with Ch'usŏk, it is not improbable that it originated as a dance of joy for an abundant harvest.

Hanshik, Cold Food Day

Hanshik, or Cold Food Day, is the one hundred fifth day after the winter solstice, which is called Tongji. On this day, Koreans clean the graves of their forebears and, of course, perform ancestral rites. And, as the name implies, they also eat cold food.

According to legend, this custom of eating cold food derived from a decree by an emperor of Ch'in China banning the kindling of fires on this day. He banned the kindling of fires on this day to show respect for an ancient Chinese statesman who chose to die in a fire rather than compromise his beliefs.

Pok-nal, Dog Days

In the lunar calendar, there are three days collectively known as Pok-nal. They are: Ch'obok, the eighth day of the sixth lunar month; Chungbok, the eighteenth day of the sixth lunar month; and, Malbok, the ninth day of the seventh lunar month. These are thought to be the three hottest times of the year.

It is customary to try to beat the heat on these days by eating such things as watermelon, and dog soup *(poshin t'ang)* and chicken-ginseng soup *(samgye t'ang)*, which are considered highly effective health rejuvenators (*see* Traditional Medicine in Lifestyle).

Sŏl-nal, Lunar New Year's Day

The first day of the first month of the lunar calendar is Sŏl-nal, a day for families to get together to remember their roots and renew close family ties. It comes about a month or a month and a half after the January 1 New Year's Day of the Gregorian calendar.

The family gathers at the *k'ŭnjip*, the oldest male member's home, and the men, from the eldest down to little boys, pay homage to their ancestors in solemn rites called *charye* (*see* Ancestral Rites in Beliefs and Customs). After the rites, formal New Year's obeisance called *sebae* (*see* New Year's Obeisance in Beliefs and Customs) is made with deep bows to the elders of the family in the order of grandparents, parents, uncles and aunts. The family then eats the food that was offered to the ancestors during the ancestral rites. The younger members then go around the village or neighborhood visiting and making deep bows to relatives and village elders.

Ttŏkkuk, a rice-dumpling soup, is traditionally eaten on Sŏl-nal. Kite-flying and playing a backgammon-like game called *yut* and a jumping seesaw-like game called *nŏlttwigi* (*see* entries in Games and Sports) are favorite Sŏl-nal pastimes.

Traditionally, people dressed in new clothes specifically prepared for Sŏl-nal as a symbol of beginning life afresh. The clothes were called *sŏlbim*. It was also customary to take all kinds of measures to ward off evil spirits and to bring good fortune.

Taeborŭm, First Full Moon Day

The fifteenth day of the first lunar month is Taeborŭm, the first full moon of the year. It marks the start of the farming season when farmers put away the games they have enjoyed since New Year's and begin preparations for seeding.

There are many customs and traditions associated with Taeborŭm, most of them aimed at seeking good health and happiness, expelling misfortune, and praying for a good harvest. Nuts (peanuts, chestnuts, hickory nuts, pine nuts and gingko nuts) are eaten on arising in the morning in the belief they will strengthen the teeth and prevent tumors. A glass of cold wine, called *kwibalki sul,* meaning "wine that sharpens the ears," is drunk with the nuts in the belief it will make the ears sharp and they will hear good news. To prepare for summer, one gives away his heat: that is, one calls someone's name and, upon their response, says *"Nae tŏwi!"*, meaning "my heat," and they will suffer the caller's heat in summer.

The highlight of Taeborŭm is viewing the full moon. In the countryside, people climb a mountain in the rear of their village to view the moon. Villagers usually compete with each other to be the first to reach the top of the mountain in the belief that the first person to see the full moon will be blessed with good luck. It is also a time to say one's wishes to the moon.

Ogokpap, literally meaning "five-grain rice," and *yakshik,* are traditionally eaten on Taeborŭm. *Ogokpap* is glutinous rice cooked together with millet *(cho),* red beans *(p'at),* sorghum *(susu),* and large beans *(pulk'ong). Yakshik* is steamed glutinous rice flavored with sugar, sesame oil, cinnamon, chestnuts, pinenuts and jujubes.

Tano, Fifth Day of Fifth Moon

The fifth day of the fifth lunar month is Tano. Falling during a lull in the busy farming season, between the planting of rice seedlings and their transfer to the paddies, Tano is a time to make merry with singing, dancing and sport.

Wrestling and swinging are two activities traditionally associated with Tano. In the past, the highlight of Tano was the *ssirŭm* (Korean wrestling; *see* entry in Games and Sports) matches to choose the Changsa, or Super Strong Man, with the lucky winner receiving an ox, which was no small prize as a good ox was essential to a farmer's livelihood. Women competed in stand-up swinging to go as high as possible with the winner receiving a gold ring. Masked dances and farmers' music and dance (*see* entries in Music and Dance) were also enjoyed.

Tano was also a time to do various things to promote good health, prepare for the summer heat, and protect against evil spirits. Tutelary deities within the home and those of the community were honored with shamanic rites to ensure their good services. Talismans to fight disease or to repel evil spirits were hung on the door or a column of the house and a bundle of freshly cut mugwort was placed beside one's gate to prevent evil spirits from entering the house. It was customary to wash one's hair with water boiled with sweet flag leaves to make it lustrous and sweet smelling. Women also wore hairpins made of sweet flag roots. The hairpins were often engraved with the Chinese characters for longevity and happiness and colored with red rouge in the belief the red color would repel evil spirits.

Tano was also a time for "marrying the jujube tree." That is, at noon on Tano, a stone was placed between the branches of a jujube tree to symbolize its marriage in the hope it would bear abundant fruit.

During the Chosŏn period (1392-1910), it was customary for the king to present fans to ranking officials in preparation for the summer heat.

The special food for the day was wheel-shaped rice cakes cooked with mugwort leaves. In addition to its medicinal properties, mugwort was also thought to have magical properties.

ARTS AND CRAFTS

Calligraphy, *Sŏye*

Although Korean and Chinese are very different languages, Koreans used Chinese characters for writing from around the second or third century and, even after the invention of the Korean alphabet (*see Han-gŭl* in Language and Letters) in 1446, Chinese continued to be used as the official script until the late nineteenth century. Thus, Korean calligraphers wrote, and most still do, in Chinese rather than Korean.

While Korea has a long history of calligraphy, not many early examples have survived the many foreign invasions and internal conflicts the country has experienced. What is known of ancient calligraphic styles and traditions has been learned from woodblock prints and handwritten copies of Buddhist scriptures, and epitaphs on stone monuments, memorial stupas for revered Buddhist monks, and other temple monuments. Generally observed, Korean calligraphy was affected by contemporary Chinese writing styles.

Calligraphy, or *sŏye* in Korean, flourished during the Chosŏn period (1392-1910) when Confucianism became the philosophy of the state and calligraphy was regarded as a necessary process of mental discipline for a cultured gentleman. A gentleman of accomplishment was expected to excel in poetry, calligraphy and painting which were considered ideal means for a Confucian-educated man to express his pure and noble mind. To combine all three he needed only an ink stick, a stone for grinding ink, animal-hair brushes and paper, collectively known as the "four friends of the scholar." Great care was taken in selecting and maintaining the "four friends," or "four stationery treasures" as they were also known, because they were considered a measure of the owner's own aesthetic taste.

Each Chinese character is composed of a number of different shaped lines within an imaginary square that are intended to convey a specific meaning. Thus, technically, calligraphy depends on the skill of the writer to create brush strokes of an interesting shape and to combine them to create beautiful structures. The writer must do this without any retouching or shading and with well-balanced spaces between brush strokes. A finished work is hung on the wall to be admired in the same way a painting is admired: Each stroke is praised for its own attributes, the ink for its tone and the whole composition for its configuration, use of space, strength and so on.

There are many styles of calligraphic writing. The most popular are: *haesŏ*, a square or printing style; *ch'osŏ*, a cursive writing style which is also known as "running grass"; *haengsŏ*, a semicursive style; and *chŏnsŏ* and *yesŏ*, two ornate writing styles.

Celadon, *Ch'ŏngja*

Ch'ŏngja, porcelaneous stoneware with a fine bluish-green glaze known in the West by the French term celadon, was the predominant ceramic ware in Korea during the Koryŏ Kingdom from the tenth century to the end of the fourteenth. It was used in court circles and in Buddhist temples.

Koryŏ celadon is considered by many to be Korea's greatest artistic achievement. Connoisseurs the world over consider it to be one of the most subtle, highly developed and technically advanced branches of the ceramic arts.

The celadon technique was first introduced to Korea in the form of Sung Chinese ceramics in the late tenth century. But Koryŏ potters did not strive to emulate the technical perfection of the Sung wares. A warm humanity pervaded their works as they turned the straight lines of Sung pottery into curves and the cold blue of Sung celadon into a soft greenish tone that was so beautiful it even became the envy of the Chinese.

Shapes and ornamental schemes were initially straightforward and subdued, taken essentially from models found in the vegetable and animal kingdoms, but with time they became increasingly elaborate so that by the twelfth century, underglaze copper and iron decoration was prevalent. Toward the middle of the twelfth century, an inlay technique called *sanggam* came into use. Decorative motifs included arabesque patterns, clouds and cranes, birds, butterflies, small grasses, water fowl, peonies, lotus, chrysanthemums and plum blossoms.

Mongol invasions that began in the thirteenth century dealt a crushing blow to Koryŏ pottery. Slight changes in firing methods, vessel shapes and decorative patterns occurred. Designs became simplified and stylized and mechanical stamping of designs was introduced. The color of inlaid celadon became greyish blue, grey or even light brown because of poor firing. The deterioration of inlaid celadon led to the development of another type of ceramics called *punch'ŏng* (*see* entry in this chapter).

Folding Screens, *Pyŏngp'ung*

Some of Korea's loveliest art is embodied in the screens, *pyŏngp'ung*, that were used by all classes of society in the past and are still a common household article.

While some screens with certain motifs were used inside and outside the house on special occasions such as weddings, birthdays, ancestral rites and funerals, most were used to enhance the interior of the home with colorful decorations embodying auspicious symbolism and happy themes. In winter, they were set up in front of windows to block drafts; hence the name *pyŏngp'ung*, meaning "windbreak."

Most Korean screens have eight panels, although two-, four-, six-, ten- and twelve-panel ones are not uncommon. The most typical type has a separate composition on each panel, the paintings being related by theme. Others have continuous or semi-continuous compositions across all the panels.

Ho, Sobriquet

Traditional-style paintings are usually stamped with the chop of the artist and signed with either the artist's sobriquet or legal name or both. The sobriquet, or *ho* in Korean, is usually put before the legal name in the signature.

The practice of using a *ho* in addition to or in lieu of one's ordinary name is believed to have begun more than two thousand years ago when the Chinese writing system was introduced to Korea. A *ho* generally consists of two very expressive Chinese characters chosen to symbolize one's self-image, creed, ideals and aspirations. It is not uncommon for an artist's *ho* to be derived from that of his teacher or mentor.

Unlike the legal name which can only be used in combination with an honorific, a title, or both when addressing someone, a *ho* can be used alone. *Ho* also help to distinguish one person from another as many Koreans have the same legal name or similar ones.

Hwagak, Ox Horn

Bright flower, bird and animal designs dominated by an orange-red background characterize *hwagak,* a decorating technique using back-painted ox horn. The term is a combination of the Chinese characters *hwa,* meaning "picture" or "lustrous," and *gak,* meaning "horn."

Horn is soaked in warm water to soften it, then pressed into flat sheets, peeled into thin layers, cut into square or rectangular panels, and polished to make it transparent. Designs are painted on what would be the back of each panel, with the accents done first and the colors added on top of them. Each panel is glued to the prepared piece, painted side in. When the glue is dry, the panels are ground and polished.

In the past, *hwagak* items were usually made for the women's quarters *(anch'ae)* where loud colors and happy, auspicious motifs were the norm. Due to the size of the horn sheets, most *hwagak* items were small, such as needle holders, spools, brush holders, jewel boxes and cosmetic cases. For larger pieces, such as chests, horn sheets were placed together like tiles, each sheet painted with an independent picture or pattern.

Hwagak appears to be a technique unique to Korea. It can be traced to the development of mother-of-pearl during the Koryŏ

Kingdom (918-1392).

Kimch'i Pots

The generic English term for the wide assortment of crocks that function as an all-purpose pantry/refrigerator is *kimch'i* pot; the Korean term is *onggi, hang-ari* or *tok.* They were and are used to store *kimch'i* (*see* Food in Lifestyle), soy sauce, soybean paste, red pepper paste, grains, water and other food items.

In size, they traditionally range from less than 6 inches to as tall as 6 feet. However, 2 to 3 feet is standard. In color, they range from dark brown to rust to ochre.

They are made on a kick-wheel but, instead of being thrown, they are made of coils of kneaded clay. Traditionally, they are glazed with a mixture of wood ash and water and baked in a wood-burning, funnel-shaped kiln which extends up a hillside. However, in recent years, more and more potters have been switching to lead-based glazes and oil in an effort to compete with cheap plastic goods.

Maedŭp, Ornamental Knots

Maedŭp, the Korean word for "knot," is the generic term for a wide assortment of knot creations often mistakenly referred to in English as macrame. *Maedŭp* and macrame are very different; the front and back of a *maedŭp* piece are identical in appearance whereas the front and back of a macrame piece are different. This is because a *maedŭp* piece comprises a knot or series of knots made of a single piece of cord whereas a macrame piece comprises a knot or series of knots made of two or more cords.

A *maedŭp* creation is usually made of silk cord, though cords of cotton and other fibers may be used. The item to be made and its use determine the type of cord and the type and number of knots to be used and their combination. There are more than thirty basic knot configurations with colorful names like dragon-fly, lotus bud, plum blossom, chrysanthemum, ginger and tortoise. Tassels or *sul* with such descriptive names as strawberry, octopus, and phoenix are often incorporated in a design to enhance its beauty.

Maedŭp was introduced to Korea from China but it was further developed into a unique system of color and design which was integral to day-to-day life. Royal and official demand for cords and *maedŭp* products was so great during the Chosŏn period (1392-1910) that an assembly line-like system with specialized artisans was operated by the government to produce them.

As can be seen in mural paintings of the Three Kingdoms period (57 B.C.-A.D. 935) and paintings of the Chosŏn period, *maedŭp* was used not only for such personal accessories as purses, perfume bags, folding fans and belts but also for interior decoration, the decoration of musical instruments, the embellishment of Buddhist pennants and more. One of the most beautiful applications of *maedŭp* was the *norigae,* a harmonious blend of knots, jewels and tassels which women wore, and many still do, to embellish the simple lines of the *hanbok* (*see* Dress in Lifestyle), the traditional Korean dress. Another common, yet striking, application was the *yuso,* a rather long piece comprising many knot configurations and generally ending in a tassel. *Yuso* were traditionally used within the home to decorate paintings, scrolls, bamboo blinds, mosquito nets and screens.

Mother-of-Pearl Lacquerware, *Chagae*

Inlaying lacquer with mother-of-pearl has been a well-known Korean specialty for centuries and remains a popular luxury item in Korea today.

The technique of inlaying lacquer came to Korea from China, possibly during the Unified Shilla period (668-935) when Korea was greatly influenced by T'ang Chinese culture. It was most popular during the Koryŏ period (918-1392) when a special office was operated by the court for the production and development of lacquerware inlaid with mother-of-pearl. Red lacquer was often decorated with inlay but black lacquer was more usual.

Lacquerware is produced by plastering hemp cloth on wooden objects and applying numerous coats of lacquer mixed with charcoal powder and rice glue. When dry, the surface is ground smooth before it is carved and inlaid with pieces of shell. After the inlaying, the surface is lacquered and ground repeatedly to obtain a smooth, lustrous surface.

The quality of mother-of-pearl ware is dependent on the design and on the luster of the shells. Abalone is considered the best for its translucent qualities.

Mulberry Paper, *Hanji*

Hanji, which literally means "Korean paper," is a term generally used for paper made of mulberry pulp. Because of its sturdiness, it has been used for centuries in many ways other than writing paper (*see* Paper Craft in this chapter).

Hanji is made by first steaming mulberry stalks. This is done so that the bark can be peeled off easily. The bark is then soaked in cold water until it becomes soft. The fibers of the white inner skin are removed from the outer skin and boiled in a mixture of water and lye. After boiling, the fibers are rinsed with cool water to remove the lye, beaten, put in a vat of cold water mixed with glue, and stirred vigorously. A fine rectangular screen is dipped into the mixture. It is moved back and forth to let the liquid pulp filter out until a thin layer remains in the screen. This layer of fibers is placed on a flat wood or stone surface to dry into a sheet of paper. The surface on which the layer of fibers is placed is often heated from beneath.

Paper Craft

Because of its sturdiness, Korean paper, called *hanji* (*see* entry in this chapter), has been used for centuries in many ways other than writing paper. It was, and still is, used to cover floors and latticed windows and doors. Oiled paper was used to make umbrellas, rain hats and fans. Strips of paper were rolled into paper cords and woven into a great variety of wares including bowls, baskets, lanterns, jars and even wash basins, chamber pots, shoes and clothes. Boxes, chests, sewing kits and more were made by pasting layer after layer of paper on both sides of a pre-fabricated framework.

Basically, there are three methods of papercrafting: papier-mâché; weaving with paper cords; and pasting layer after layer of paper to form a shape, sometimes with the use of a prefabricated frame. Items are lacquered or colored with natural dyes and for furniture items metal hinges and other accessories are added. Items are decorated with colored paper adroitly cut in symmetrical patterns.

Pojagi, Wrapping Cloths

Wrapping cloths and covers called *pojagi* have been an indispensable household item in Korea since ancient times. Also called *po, pok, poja* and *pojaegi,* they were, and still are, used for wrapping many things including clothes, bedding, and precious articles to store and protect them from dust, for covering tables and trays of food to protect them from flies and insects, and to wrap bundles and packages for easy carrying. One reason for the enduring popularity of *pojagi* is that they can be used for wrapping and storing large bundles but when not in use can be folded up very small for easy storage.

Pojagi are usually very colorful and generally made of cotton, satin, silk or ramie. They are generally decorated with geometric patterns made of scraps of cloth or with embroidered designs

embodying a wish for long life, happiness or good fortune. They
vary in size and thickness depending on their purpose. Some
have ties and some do not. Those used to cover food are often
lined with waxed paper.

In ancient times, *pojagi* were used by commoners and royalty
alike. However, those used in common households were multi-
purpose whereas those used within the court were made for an
express purpose.

Punch'ŏng

Punch'ŏng was the predominant ceramic ware from around 1392
until the 1590s. It was produced in large quantities for everyday
use by commoners but it was also used at the royal court.

Punch'ŏng glaze is of a celadon type, the name meaning "pale
blue green." When thick enough and fired at the proper degree
of reduction, it looks exactly like the Koryŏ celadon from which
it developed.

However, during the Chosŏn period (1392-1910), the production of great quantities precluded the precise firing and reduction
necessary to achieve the blue-green color characteristic of Koryŏ
celadon. The grey clay used for *punch'ŏng* was similar to that used
in Koryŏ celadon, but coarser in texture. The identifying characteristic of *punch'ŏng* was an overall white slip decoration.

The most typical kind of decoration was a stamped-and-inlaid
technique. Designs were stamped in the surface of the leather-
hard clay after a piece was thrown and trimmed and then white
slip was painted on. After the slip set, the slip was scraped away,
leaving the stamped designs filled with white clay. Other techniques included brushing with slip, dipping in slip, painting
black slip designs over white slip and painting the surface with
slip and then carving away the slip to produce a design.

Sagunja, Four Noble Gentlemen Painting

In the realm of literati painting, that is the painting Confucian-trained scholar-officials of Chosŏn (1392-1910) did for their own amusement and edification, plum, orchid, chrysanthemum, and bamboo are collectively known as *sagunja,* the Four Noble Gentlemen.

For the scholar official, the plum, which blooms in the cold at the end of winter, represented the wisdom which the scholar-official could offer even in the winter of his life. The orchid, which grows wild in the mountains and has a faint fragrance, represented the refined thoughts of the scholar which should be appreciated like the orchid's noble fragrance. The chrysanthemum, which blooms in autumn, represented a productive prime of life. Bamboo, which bends but does not break in the wind, represented the noble gentleman who, like the bamboo, bends but does not break in the face of adversity.

In other words, the four represent courage and strength, nobleness, productivity and integrity.

Shipchangsaeng, Ten Longevity Symbols

Shipchangsaeng is the Korean term for ten *(ship)* animals, plants and objects that symbolize longevity. The Taoist inspired *shipchangsaeng* is one of the most frequently encountered motifs in Korea. It is a favorite theme for paintings, screens, holiday greeting cards, spoon and chopstick pouches and other household objects.

The ten animals, plants and objects are rocks, mountains, water, clouds, pine trees, the Fungus of Immortality *(pulloch'o),* tortoises, deer, cranes and the sun. The appropriateness of the sun, clouds, water and rocks is pretty apparent as they appear to last indefinitely.

Pine trees suggest longevity because a pine normally lives a long time, is always green and is resistant to the elements. The

Fungus of Immortality, or Sacred Fungus, is a magic mushroom that grows in the Land of the Immortals and brings eternal life to those who eat it.

Cranes and deer are the companions and messengers of the Taoist Immortals and thus symbolize longevity and immortality. As sea turtles do live for centuries, the symbolism is less mythical. The Taoist tortoise, which is said to live ten thousand years, is the messenger of the Dragon King who dwells at the bottom of the sea.

Tanch'ŏng

Tanch'ŏng is the generic name for the colorful patterns that emblazon the exposed woodwork inside and outside many traditional structures, especially temples. The name is derived from the Chinese characters for red and blue, its two major colors, which Koreans pronounce *tan* and *ch'ŏng*.

Though not apparent at first glance, there is a definite sequence to the colors comprising the patterns. The sequence follows a code derived from Buddhist symbolism and cosmology. The elements embody protective and fortuitous symbols as well as represent heaven, earth and the cycle of reincarnation.

The painting of the patterns involves many steps. First an overall design is made and then a cartoon or master drawing of it is made. Paper transfer sheets are then made for duplicating the various design components onto the building.

To make the transfer sheets, half of the part to be duplicated is drawn on a piece of heavy paper that has been folded in half. The outline of the drawing and all its parts are pricked with a pin. The paper is then unfolded, revealing the outline of the whole design.

The perforated transfer sheet is held against the part of the building to be painted and struck with a cloth bag filled with powdered chalk. The paper is then removed to reveal a dotted white outline of the pattern. Of course, the surface to be adorned should be primed prior to this last step to seal the wood and provide a base on which colors can be easily painted. The primer is a greenish-blue coating made of dark green mineral powder, white powder made of crushed sea shells and a wheat starch binder.

The colors, which are opaque, soluble in water and do not mix easily with one another, are made from finely ground mineral particles. The dry pigments are mixed with a heated mixture of animal glue and water that serves as an adhesive.

The heating of the glue is crucial, for heating too much or too little can affect the quality of the colors and their fluidity. The mix must be kept warm to remain liquid and stored under water to be kept workable. These colors, as well as the primer mentioned earlier, are highly poisonous and thus protect the wood from damage by insects and other organisms.

The hot colors, first the light and then the dark, are applied to the prepared areas. The designs are finished with black and white outlines to define the patterns. Camellia oil is painted over the finished *tanch'ŏng* to protect it from the weather.

The mineral pigments, the painting techniques and much of the iconography of *tanch'ŏng* were brought to Korea from China. However, Korean artists added their own special touches, many of them humorous.

White Porcelain, *Paekcha*

Paekcha is the Korean name for the white porcelain wares that were made throughout the Chosŏn period (1392-1910). It was for the court and aristocracy whereas *punch'ŏng* (*see* entry in this chapter), which was produced concurrently during the early years of the period, was for the masses. *Paekcha* satisfied the prevailing Confucian ethic which demanded wares of a simpler nature than the elaborate and richly decorated wares of the previous Koryŏ Kingdom (918-1392).

Early *paekcha* is characterized by robust form, thick potting and opaque whiteness. Later pieces have a wide tonal range including greyish white, bluish white, milky white and pure white.

White porcelain with cobalt-blue decorations was made from the mid-fifteenth century. Inlaid white porcelain was also made by carving designs in the white clay, filling the depressions with reddish brown clay and applying white porcelain glaze on the surface; the designs turned black when fired. White porcelain with underglaze painting in brown iron oxide was made from the fifteenth century but became quite prevalent in the seventeenth century along with underglaze red decorations. Both techniques were used in the eighteenth century, sometimes in combination. White porcelain with underglaze copper designs was produced in quantity in the late Chosŏn period.

MUSIC AND DANCE

Buddhist Ritual Dance, *Chakpŏp*

Korean Buddhism has three basic ritual dances that are collectively called *chakpŏp*. They are: *nabich'um* (butterfly dance), a prayer dance in which cherubs and angels symbolically descend from heaven; *parach'um* (cymbal dance), a prayer dance by cherubs who play large cymbals while they dance; and *pŏpkoch'um* (drum dance), a dance in which the tribulations of the dead are symbolically relieved by the beating of a large barrel drum. Each of the dances has variants and shares a limited number of dance movements.

The *nabich'um* is usually performed by one dancer dressed in a white robe with very wide and deep long trailing sleeves and an embroidered peak hat.

The *parach'um* is usually performed by two or four dancers. While twisting their bodies in spiral turns, the dancers swing the large cymbals (*para*) to and fro, deftly revolving them rapidly in spirals, and softly clashing them one on top of the other.

The *pŏpkoch'um* begins with a dramatic rolling of the drum sticks around the ridges of the drum's circumference and gradually building up to a crescendo of passionate drumming. Traditionally performed by one dancer, the popularized stage version may be performed by any number of dancers on as many small stand drums. The dance combines rhythmic dexterity with acrobatic movement.

The three dances are danced to chants whose purpose is to prepare for or to celebrate death and the release of the soul into paradise. Musical accompaniment is provided by a band called *chorach'i* or *kyŏngnaech'wi* that consists of one or two *t'aepyŏngso* (conical oboe), *ching* (large gong), *puk* (double-headed barrel drum), *para* (cymbals), *nabal* (long trumpet), and *nagak* (conch shell horn). Members of the band are usually lay musicians though the ritual chant singers and the dancers are Buddhist monks.

Chinese and Japanese Buddhism have no similar dances.

Buddhist Ritual Music

Buddhist ritual music, which includes chants and instrumental music, varies according to its role in a given rite. The chants are far more important than the instrumental music.

There are three types of ritual chants: *yŏmbul*, the reciting of sutras; *hwach'ŏng*, chanting based on a folksong style; and *pŏmp'ae*, a long solemn chant. (*See yŏmbul, hwach'ŏng* and *pomp'ae* in this chapter.)

Ch'anggŭk, Folk Opera

Ch'anggŭk can be defined as a folk opera employing *p'ansori* artists *(see P'ansori* in this chapter) to play the various characters. The singers wear costumes and make-up and stage props, scenery, lighting and sound effects are employed.

Ch'anggŭk developed from *p'ansori* around the beginning of the twentieth century. It has become increasingly popular in recent years. Most presentations are adaptations of *p'ansori*.

Chinese Court Music, *Tang-ak*

Tang-ak, litearally meaning "music of the T'ang Dynasty," refers to secular music of the Chinese T'ang (618-906) and Sung (960-1279) dynasties which, after its introduction to Korea, was altered to use in court functions such as royal banquets.

The term *tang-ak* was originated during the Shilla period (57 B.C.-A.D. 935) to indicate music of T'ang Chinese origin that was used in the Korean court from the seventh century, thereby differentiating it from the music existing in Korea prior to the rise of the T'ang Dynasty. During the Koryŏ period (918-1392), the term was broadened to include all Chinese music which had come into Korea during and after the T'ang Dynasty.

Classical Music, *Kug-ak*

Korean classical music is called *kug-ak*. It is based on triple time and is clearly different from the duple-time music of neighboring cultures. It can sound lilting, droning and haunting.

Kug-ak embodies a wide variety of musical forms. Some sources categorize *kug-ak* into music for the court and aristocracy (*chǒng-ak*), and music for the folk or common man (*minsog-ak* or *sog-ak*) while others categorize it into court, folk and religious. For convenience it is presented under the following headings:

Buddhist Music
Chinese Music, *Tang-ak*
Confucian Shrine Music, *Munmyo-ak*
Court Music, *A-ak*
Farmer's Music and Dance, *Nong-ak*
Folk Music, *Minsog-ak*
Korean Court Music, *Hyang-ak*
Processional Music, *Koch'wi*
Royal Ancestral Shrine Music, *Chongmyo-ak*
Shamanic Music, *Shinawi*

Confucian Dance, *Ilmu*

Ilmu, the dances performed during Confucian ceremonies, are not dances in the conventional sense. They are a series of simple ritual movements to add emphasis to the ceremonial offerings and to usher the spirits of the dead to the feast. The dances comprise a civil dance, *munmu*, and a military dance, *mumu*.

The dances are performed in rigid lines by dancers clad in scarlet robes and black felt boots. They involve very little movement from place to place. They consist primarily of circular arm movements and bows to the cardinal points. The dances are distinguishable by the hats the dancers wear and the objects they carry. During the civil dance, each dancer wears a stiff black, flat-topped, rectangular hat and carries a feathered stick with a dragon head in his left hand and a bamboo flute in his right hand. During the military dance, each dancer wears a red, flat-topped, cone-shaped hat and holds a small wooden shield in his left hand and a small wooden hammer in his right.

The civil dance is performed during the ushering in of the spirit and the offering of the first cup of wine. The military dance is performed when the second and third cups of wine are offered. Traditionally the Korean dancers were divided into two parts, but they now perform in a single unit. During the time of Confucius, the rank of the person being honored determined the number of dancers; for example, sixty-four in eight lines of eight for the Son of Heaven, forty-eight in eight lines of six for a king, thirty-six in six lines of six for a lord, and sixteen in four lines of four for ranking government officials and lesser aristocrats. In Korea, the number of dancers fluctuated. Now sixty-four dancers perform in the rites for Confucius (see Confucian Shrine Music in this chapter) and thirty-six perform in the rites for royal ancestors (*see* Royal Ancestral Shrine Music in this chapter). In the past, the dances were performed by male dancers but now they are performed by female dancers.

Confucian Shrine Music, *Munmyo-ak*

The history of Confucian shrine music in Korea dates back to the twelfth century when Emperor Hui Tsung (r. 1101-1126) of Sung China sent the first Confucian ritual music and instruments together with instruments used at Chinese court banquets to the Koryŏ court in 1116. Two years later, the Emperor sent the Koryŏ court a complete set of instruments for ritual music as well as instructions in two types of ritual dance collectively known as *ilmu* (*see* Confucian Dance in this chapter).

The music is still performed twice a year in the second and eighth months of the lunar calendar at Munmyo (Temple of Confucius; *see* entry in Famous Places and Monuments). It is performed as part of the *sŏkchŏn* rites that are performed to honor Confucius (*see* Rites for Confucius in Beliefs and Customs). It is called *munmyo-ak* and falls under the category of ritual music which falls under the broader category of court music and is thus often referred to by the terms *cherye-ak*, meaning ritual music, and *a-ak*, which is sometimes used to mean ritual music and sometimes used to mean court music.

The music is performed antiphonally by two orchestras: the terrace, or *tŭngga*, orchestra situated on the terrace of the main shrine; and, the ground, or *hŏn-ga*, orchestra situated in the courtyard. The orchestras are theoretically required to include instruments which represent all of the eight materials—metal, stone, silk, bamboo, gourd, clay, leather and wood. The terrace orchestra is composed of the following instruments: *t'ŭkkyŏng* (suspended stone struck with a mallet), *t'ŭkchong* (clapperless bell struck with a mallet), *p'yŏn-gyŏng* (stone chimes), *p'yŏnjong* (bell chimes), *ch'uk* (pounded wooden box) *ŏ* (wooden scraper), *pak* (wooden clapper), *chi* (short transverse bamboo flute), *yak* (end-blown notched bamboo flute), *chŏk* (end-blown notched bamboo flute), *hun* (globular clay ocarina), *so* (panpipes), *chŏlgo* (barrel drum), *kŭm* (7-string zither), and *sŭl* (25-string zither). The ground orchestra includes all the instruments of the terrace orchestra except the *t'ŭkkyŏng*, *t'ŭkchong*, *so*, *kŭm*, and *sŭl* plus it includes a *chin-go* (large barrel drum), a *nogo* (set of 2 long barrel drums), and a *nodo* (set of 2 small barrel drums).

The music has a classical symmetry and simplicity reflecting Confucian ideals of balance and universal harmony. The melody is performed in slow tempo with uniform durations and with minimal ornamentation and dynamic change.

The music the orchestras now perform has been performed since the reign of King Sejong (r. 1418-50; *see* entry in Historic Figures). King Sejong preferred Confucian music for two types of ceremonies: the rites in which he and his officials followed ceremonial etiquette in offering food to divine spirits and the royal audiences in which he met with government officials. King Sejong had the court's music master, Pak Yŏn, restore the ritual music as near as possible to its original Chou Dynasty (1111-221 B.C.) form as it had become adulterated since its introduction from Sung China in the early twelfth century. Pak did away with compositions of questionable authenticity and adopted a new repertory from the *Taesŏng akpo (Music of the Confucian Shrine)* of China's Yüan Dynasty (1260-1368). At the same time, steps were taken to find suitable materials for the manufacture of the instruments in Korea.

Included in *The Annals of King Sejong* is a treatise on ceremonial music *(A-ak po)* which was completed by historians and musicians of Sejong's court in 1430. It describes Korean theories of ceremonial music and preserves some early Chinese ritual melodies since lost in China itself.

Court Dance, *Chŏngjae*

Chŏngjae, meaning "display of talent," refers to dances performed at court banquets. Like court music, *chongjae* can be divided into *tang-ak*, Chinese dance, and *hyang-ak*, native Korean dance.

Chinese dances were introduced to Korea during the Shilla (57 B.C.-A.D. 935) and Koryŏ (918-1392) periods and, like Chinese music at the time, were designated *tang-ak*. Very few *tang-ak* dances have survived. One of the oldest still performed is *P'ogurak* (Ball Throwing Dance). In this combination of dance and game, two teams of six girls take turns trying to throw a ball through a hole at the top of a model gate. If they succeed, they are given a flower by the "flower girl"; if they fail, they are given a black mark on the cheek by the "brush girl."

One of the best known of the traditional *hyang-ak* dances is the sword dance, *Kŏmgimu* or *Kŏmmu*. A folk dance originally, it was incorporated into the court repertoire during the Chosŏn period (1392-1910). The dance commemorates the heroic deed of Hwangch'ang, a teenage boy of Shilla, a *hwarang (see* entry in Miscellaneous chapter), who used his skill as a sword dancer to finagle his way into the presence of the enemy Paekche king and killed him.

Another *hyang-ak* is the *mugo* drum dance that is known as the Victory Dance of Ch'ungmu. In this dance, eight dancers circle around a large drum; four dancers hold flowers and four dancers have drumsticks concealed in their long sleeves (*hansam*). The dancers with the flowers approach the drum first and touch it lightly with the flowers. Then the dancers with the hidden drumsticks approach the drum and suddenly bring down their drumsticks simultaneously and beat the drum with a rousing bang. The advancing and retreating of the two circles of dancers symbolizes the movement of military formations. The dance is said to have been used by Admiral Yi Sun-shin (*see* entry in Historic Figures) to increase the morale of his troops during the 1592-98 Japanese invasions of Korea.

One of the oldest dances is the *Ch'ŏyongmu* (Dance of the Dragon of the Eastern Sea), which dates to the Shilla period. The dance celebrates the life of Ch'ŏyong, a man who came to live in Shilla from a distant land. Over the years it changed from a solo performance, to a duet, to a quintet. During the Chosŏn period, it was performed before New Year's Day to exorcise all evil from the royal court. The five dancers, each wearing a brown faced mask and wearing costumes of blue, white, red, black and yellow (signifying the four cardinal points and the center of them) perform solo turning sequences, then each dances with the center figure, and all turn in unison.

One of the most awe-inspiring dances is *Ch'unaengmu* (Dance of the Spring Nightingale), which was created by Prince Hyomyŏng (Ikchong; 1809-30) of Chosŏn. The dance is executed by a solo performer entirely within the area of a small reed mat. It is characterized by extrememly slow, delicate movements.

Other commonly performed court dances are the Flower Crown Dance, which is used to begin almost every performance of Korean dance; the Beautiful Persons Picking Peonies, which was first choreographed by Prince Hyomyŏng; and the Crane Dance, which is performed by two dancers in crane costumes.

Court Music, *A-ak*

Originally used in reference to court music of Chinese origin, the term *a-ak* has come to be used more broadly for repertories of court ritual and entertainment of both Chinese and Korean origin, *tang-ak* and *hyang-ak* (*see* individual entries). *A-ak*, which is also known by the term *chŏng-ak*, literally meaning "right music," comprises music performed at court banquets (*yŏlle-ak*), music performed in royal processions (*koch'wi*), and music performed for various rituals (*cherye-ak; see* Confucian Shrine Music and Royal Ancestral Shrine Music in this chapter).

Most court music is performed primarily by instrumental ensembles. The basic ensemble includes *p'iri* (double-reed oboe), *taegŭm* (large transverse flute), *haegŭm* (2-string fiddle) and *chang-go* (hourglass drum). The court orchestra comprises the basic ensemble plus *tanjŏk* (small transverse flute) for the high treble parts, *ajaeng* (bowed zither) for the bass parts, and *chwago* (framed barrel drum); the three melodic instruments—*p'iri*, *taegum*, and *haegum*—are usually doubled. Some pieces include *komŭn-go* (6-string zither) and *kayagŭm* (12-string zither) or *p'yŏnjong* (bell chimes) and *p'yŏn-gyŏng* (stone chimes) or both. In its fullest form the court ensemble comprises the basic ensemble plus *tanso* (vertical flute), *kayagŭm, kŏmun-go,* and *yanggŭm* (dulcimer).

A very different ensemble called *chorach'i* performs processional music (*see* Processional Music). It comprises *taep'yŏngso* (conical oboe), *nabal* (long trumpet), *nagak* (conch shell horn), *chabara* (cymbals), *ching* (large gong), and *yonggŏ* (snare drum). The *taep'yŏngso* is the sole melodic instrument and the *nabal* and *nagak* function as drones. Other ensembles are used for Confucian ritual music (*see* Confucian Shrine Music and Royal Ancestral Shrine Music in this chapter).

Court music also includes three vocal genres or *norae*: *kagok* (cyclical songs with long instrumental suites), *kasa* (narrative songs), and *shijo* (short classical poems; *see* individual entries).

Dance, *Ch'um*

There are six varieties of Korean dance: shamanic, Buddhist, Confucian, court, folk and dramatic. They all have in common the heel walk, turning on the heels, raising the body softly and lightly from a bent knee position, slight vibrations from the hips up, pulses from the shoulders, economy of movement, and improvisation. The most distinctive movement is the suspended position, balancing on one foot with the free leg extended while the shoulders softly rise and fall.

The Korean dancer seeks to express metaphysical joy—*mŏt* and *p'ung*—rather than sexuality and acrobatic physical motion.

For more about dance see the following in this chapter:

Buddhist Ritual Dance, *Chakpŏp*
Confucian Dance, *Ilmu*
Court Dance, *Chŏngja*
Fan Dance, *Puch'e Ch'um*
Farmer's Music and Dance, *Nong-ak*
Kanggangsuwŏllae
Masked Dance Drama, *T'alch'um*
Salp'uri
Sŭngmu

Fan Dance, *Puch'e Ch'um*

One of the most popular dances for stage, the Fan Dance is performed by a group of women who dance with folding fans, or *puch'e*. The dancers open and close the fans as they dance to a lighthearted, flowing rhythm. The climax of the dance is when the dancers form a large fluttering flower that appears to rotate. The dancers wear a colorful costume akin to that once worn by dancers in the royal court and a flower crown. Peony blossoms are painted on the fans.

The dance developed from a folk ritual.

Farmer's Music and Dance, *Nong-ak*

Nong-ak, literally meaning "farm music," has been traditionally associated with planting and harvesting crops. It can be traced to agricultural rituals performed before the dawn of the Three Kingdoms period (57 B.C.-A.D. 668). In the past, it was indispensable at the celebration of social and religious events such as New Year's, Buddha's Birthday, Ch'usŏk and shamanic rituals, for example, rituals to pray for a bumper crop and rituals to purify a village well.

Nong-ak is performed by a percussion band comprising *kkwaenggwari* (small gong), *changgo* (hourglass drum), *yonggo* (snare drum), and *ching* (large gong), with the optional inclusion of *taep'yŏngso* (conical oboe) and *nabal* (long trumpet). The band leader, or *sangsoe*, is the *kkwaenggwari* player. He signals rhythmic patterns to the other musicians.

The musicians wear white *hanbok* (*see* entry in Lifestyle), and brilliantly colored vests, sashes and hats. They play and dance simultaneously, improvising intricate gyrations and dance steps. The physical movement may be done in duple patterns while the music is performed in triple time and vice versa.

There are two major styles of *nong-ak*: *chwado kut*, which is performed in the eastern half of the country and the inland areas of Chŏlla-do; and, *udo kut*, which is performed in the coastal areas of the southwest. *Chwado kut* is faster than *udo kut* and the dancing is more acrobatic. Some of the performers wear hats with long paper streamers attached to the top which they set in motion by moving their heads. They twirl the streamers in large loops or figure eights while dancing and playing. *Udo kut* is slower than *chwado kut* and the rhythms are more intricate. The dancing is less acrobatic and, instead of hats with streamers, some of the dancers wear paper-flowered hats *(kkokkal)* that turn and bob with every movement of the head. Nowadays the two styles are often mixed.

Folk Music, *Minsog-ak*

Unlike court music (*see* entry in this chapter) and ritual music (*cherye-ak; see* Confucian Shrine Music, and Royal Ancestral Shrine Music in this chapter), folk music, *sog-ak* or *minsog-ak,* is full of energy and passion and is primarily vocal and performed by soloists. It includes a large number of folk songs, or *minyo,* with a great variety of subject matter, mood and tempo. There are lullabies, work songs, game songs, love songs and religious songs. The songs may be happy, sad, resigned, discontented or humorous in mood and fast or slow in tempo. Many have a refrain that is often sung by a chorus in answer to a soloist's verse and may include nonsense syllables.

Agricultural tasks such as rice planting, weeding, and harvesting are the most frequent subject of work songs. There are also pearl-diving songs, weaving songs, fishing songs, and more. For other folk music forms see the following in this chapter:

Farmer's Music and Dance, *Nong-ak*
P'ansori
Sanjo
Shamanic Music, *Shinawi*

Hwach'ŏng

Hwach'ŏng, literally meaning "humble request," is the singing of a chant by a Buddhist monk who accompanies himself between the vocal sections with a small gong struck with a mallet while another monk accompanies the chant by striking the heads and body of a *puk*, or barrel drum, suspended on a frame. The texts of the chants usually deal with the transcience of secular life, conversion to Buddhism, religious commandments, and the rewards of Buddhism.

The *hwach'ŏng* chant is based on the Korean vernacular, which makes it more easily understood by the laity, and its singing technique, vocal projection, rhythmic structure and poetic form are closely related to folk songs. These features suggest that *hwach'ŏng* possibly originated from an attempt to make Buddhism more readily understandable to common people.

Hwach'ŏng is used only in special rites, not in daily monastic services.

Kagok

Kagok is a lengthy song cycle that was enjoyed by the literati of the Chosŏn period (1392-1910). It is sung as a solo or duet with the accompaniment of a chamber ensemble. The standard accompaniment includes *kŏmun-go* (6-string zither), *taegŭm* (large transverse flute), *p'iri* (double-reed oboe), *haegŭm* (2-string fiddle) and *changgo* (hourglass drum). Sometimes *kayagŭm* (12-string long zither) and *tanso* (end-blown flute) are added to the ensemble.

All the songs in a cycle are related melodically but not textually. Each song is structurally divided into five vocal sections framed by an instrumental prelude and postlude and having an instrumental interlude between the third and the fourth. The first and last song of each cycle is always preceded by a *kŏmun-go* prelude.

The present *kagok* repertory was established in the seventeenth and eighteenth centuries and consists of twenty-seven songs.

Kanggangsuwollae

Kanggangsuwollae is a circle dance for women that is generally performed at Ch'usŏk, the Harvest Moon Festival, the fifteenth day of the eighth lunar month (*see* entry in Special Days). The dance is performed by a large group of girls to their own singing. It starts very slowly, moving clockwise and then counterclockwise around a solo singer who dances in the center of the circle, and accelerates to a rapid whirling climax. The girl in the center sings the lyrics and the other girls sing the refrain. The lyrics of the song the dancers sing express desires for happiness, longevity and love while describing typical household scenes. The refrain, *kanggangsuwollae,* means "watch or guard the surroundings."

The dance supposedly developed from a trick women played on Japanese invaders in the sixteenth century by dancing around fires in the evening to make the invaders believe their target was well defended. Some say the trick was the idea of Admiral Yi Sun-shin (*see* entry in Historic Figures) but some say the dance existed before his time. However, being traditionally associated with Ch'usŏk, it is not improbable that it originated as a dance of joy for an abundant harvest.

Kasa

Kasa is a long narrative song in strophic or through-composed form that was enjoyed by literati of the Chosŏn period (1392-1910). The standard accompaniment is *changgo* (hourglass drum). However, it is sometimes accompanied by an ensemble of *changgo*, *p'iri* (double-reed oboe), *haegŭm* (large transverse flute), and *haegŭm* (2-string fiddle). The accompaniment of the instruments is not prescribed, they merely follow the melody with ornamentation and fill in the vocal pauses. The rhythmic pattern of each song is based on a five- or six-pulse rhythm.

The singer, female as well as male, switches back and forth between normal voice and falsetto, a change not found in other Korean vocal art songs of the court and literati tradition. The singer draws out the syllables of the text to such an extent that the meaning of the song is lost unless one can actually see the words.

Korean Court Music, *Hyang-ak*

Hyang-ak refers to court music of early Korean origin, Chinese music that came to Korea before the T'ang Dynasty (618-906) and compositions of the Koryŏ (918-1392) and Chosŏn (1392-1910) periods. The term means "native music."

Masked Dance Drama, *T'alch'um*

T'alch'um is the generic name for a group of satirical dance dramas performed by dancers wearing masks. The word is a combination of *t'al*, meaning "mask," and *ch'um*, meaning "dance."

The masked dance dramas have no story line or plot running through them. They are a series of satirical vignettes, independent of each other, portraying, for example, the foibles and misadventures of an apostate Buddhist monk, a lecherous aristocrat, a stupid nobleman and his clever servant, a traveling salesman and a charlatan shaman. The whole spectrum of ancient society's conflicts between ages, sexes and classes are dramatized with comic dialogues, pantomime, intermittent singing and dancing.

The extant masked dance dramas can be classified into three groups: *sŏnang*, ritual plays that were part of seasonal provincial rites which included rites at the spirit shrine and rites in which exorcism was important; *Sandae togam*, plays that were managed by a government office of the same name during the early Chosŏn period (1392-1910) but were banned at court in 1634 and eventually came to be associated with provincial urban centers; and, *sajagye*, lion mask plays that can be traced to China, where the lion was venerated as a Bodhisattva, and other parts of central and south Asia. The lion mask play had appeared in Korea by the time of Shilla (57 B.C.-A.D. 935). The Korean lion was believed to be capable of driving evil spirits out of households as the dance procession wound its way round the village prior to the beginning of a performance. Apart from the scenes in which the lion dances, eats his rival, and is cured of his subsequent indigestion, the scenes are similar to those of the *sŏnang*.

Masked dance drama was a way for commoners to release their frustrations about their treatment by the upper classes and the clergy and to laugh at themselves.

Musical Instruments, *Akki*

Sixty different kinds of traditional musical instruments (*akki*) are known in Korea. About forty-five of them are still used.

The instruments can be classified in several different ways. One system, which was developed by Korean music theorists during the early Chosŏn period (1392-1910), groups instruments according to the musical genre in which they are used. Another system, which was developed much earlier in China and applied mainly to instruments used to perform court ritual music, groups them into the eight categories of metal, stone, silk, bamboo, gourd, clay, leather and wood. And still another, more modern method is to group them in the categories of chordophone, aerophone, idiophone, and membranophone. Here the instruments are grouped under the headings Percussion Instruments, String Instruments, and Wind Instruments.

P'ansori

P'ansori is best defined as a narrative-epic-dramatic folk vocal art form performed by one singer accompanied by one drummer playing one drum. As to the etymology of the word *p'ansori*, it is generally believed that *p'an* indicates a place or area for the performing of various folk arts and *sori* means "sound," both spoken and sung. Thus, *p'ansori* can be roughly translated song (or songs) sung at a place of entertainment.

P'ansori is sung by one singer, male or female, to the accompaniment of a drummer who plays a small barrel-shaped drum (*puk*) by striking the drum head with his left palm and the wooden barrel of the drum with a stick held in his right hand. The singer, generally holding a folding fan and a handkerchief and sitting or standing at the center of the stage, delivers a well-known folk tale with singing (*sori*), recitation (*aniri*), and body expressions (*pallim*). The drummer, usually sitting to the left of the singer, accompanies the singer with rhythmic cycles, varying their patterns and tempo in accordance with the mood or melodic progression of the song and makes suitable calls of encouragement (*ch'uimsae*) at appropriate phrase endings to inspire the singer, which also excites the audience. The drummer's role is so important that it is said a *p'ansori* singer cannot be good without a good drummer.

The origin of *p'ansori* is highly disputed but the general concensus is that its melodic roots can be traced to shamanistic ritual songs of the Chŏlla region. It is thought that the men who provided the musical accompaniment for shamans abandoned their religious functions to become *kwangdae*, something like bards or minstrels. They traveled around the countryside in troupes to perform at villages. Their repertoire came to include juggling, tumbling and tightrope walking as well as music and dance. Between performances, they told stories drawn from well-known folk tales, employing both recitations and songs, the melodic structures of the songs being drawn from regional folk songs and shamanistic ritual music. The stories and songs were recited and sung entirely by rote as the performers had no formal education.

The date *p'ansori* became independent of the entertainment offered at village gathering places is not known. However, it seems to have developed to such a point that its practitioners disassociated themselves from the acrobats around the middle of the Chosŏn period (1392-1910). It then began to appeal to aristocrats, who until then had disdained it as befitting only the lower classes. From the nineteenth century, *p'ansori* singers began to be patronized by the nobility. Consequently, many vulgarities were dropped from the texts and many quotes from Chinese classics were incorporated. As its popularity spread among the nobility, the singers' circumstances improved as they were presented honorariums of rice or money. Some singers devoted their whole lives to *p'ansori* and developed personalized performing styles which they passed on to later generations of singers.

P'ansori were first put in written form by Shin Chae-hyo (1812-84), a literati from an aristocratic family in Koch'ang, Chŏllabuk-do Province. Shin not only compiled five *p'ansori*, he refined and polished them. He also influenced the way in which they were performed by arranging the texts with more appropriate rhythms and melodic patterns and improved singing, reciting and gesturing techniques, which served to make the pieces hold together more like a drama in the modern sense of the word. In the process, he trained many singers including the first female *p'ansori* singer. His work, especially his innovations, contributed to *p'ansori* becoming a stage art and the subsequent development around the beginning of the twentieth century of *ch'anggŭk* (*see* entry in this chapter), a folk opera employing *p'ansori* artists.

Records show that until the early nineteenth century, there were twelve *p'ansori*. Now only the five Shin compiled are known in their entirety. The lyrics but not the music of four others are also known. Each *p'ansori* generally takes six to eight hours to perform in its entirety so they are now usually performed in one- to two-hour abbreviated versions. A libretto is often provided to help audiences understand the story.

Percussion Instruments

Chabara Thin circular brass cymbals related to the Chinese *bo, chabara* are also known as *para* and *chegŭm*. In historical records they are referred to as *tongbal, hyangbal, yobal,* and *pal.*

There is no standard size and pres- ent usage is limited. The largest and heaviest, called *para,* are used in Buddhist ceremonial dances. The smallest, called *hyang-bal,* are fastened to the thumbs and middle fingers of dancers and used like castanets. The large ones are also used in military processional music, *koch'wi* (*see* Processional Music in this chapter), and in shamanistic rituals of the northwest style they replace the bronze gong, *ching.*

They are held by cloth handles attached to holes in the center and played by being struck together.

Changgo The chief percussion instrument of Korea, the *changgo* is a double-headed drum shaped like an hourglass. The name comes from *chang,* meaning "stick," and *go,* meaning "drum." It is known by a variety of names: *sŏlchanggo* in farmer's music (*see*

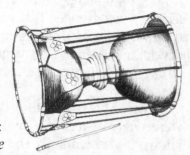

Farmer's Music and Dance in this chapter); *seyogo* in historical sources; and *changgu* in central Korea.

The instrument is made in a number of sizes ranging in length from roughly 40 centimeters to over 60 centimeters and in diameter at the ends from roughly 20 centimeters to over 30 centimeters. The body of the drum is made of a single piece of paulownia wood carved in the shape of an hourglass and is hollow even at the narrow waist. It is often painted red, though some used in *nong-ak* are left natural. The circular heads of animal skin are mounted on metal hoops slightly larger than the diameter of the ends of the wooden body. The two heads are laced to each other by cords running from hooks on the metal hoops. Small leather sleeves on pairs of adjacent cords can be manipulated to adjust the head tension. Ancient records show that both heads were originally of horseskin, thin on the right and thick on the left, but now the right is usually of dogskin or sheepskin and the left of cowhide, except for the drums used in *nong-ak* which have dogskin for both heads.

In most types of music the instrument is placed horizontally on the floor in front of the seated performer. The left side is struck with the palm of the left hand to produce a low, soft sound and the right side is struck with a slim bamboo stick to produce a hard, crisp sound. In *nong-ak,* which requires considerable volume because it is generally performed outdoors, the performer holds a bamboo mallet with a ball of wood at the tip in his left hand, hitting both the right and left heads, and a sturdy bamboo stick in his right hand, striking the center of the right skin in a virtuoso technique.

The instrument has a long history in Korea. It appears in paintings from the Koguryŏ period (37 B.C.-A.D. 668) and in artifacts from the Shilla period (57 B.C.-A.D. 935). At present it is found in most genres of Korean music. Its main purpose is to articulate the repetitions of structural rhythmic patterns as an accompaniment to melody instruments. However, there is also a solo repertory of considerable rhythmic subtlety in *nong-ak.*

Ching The *ching* is a large, flat, lipped bronze gong which is also called *taegŭm* (large gong), *kŭm* (gong), *na* (gong), and *kŭmna* (metal gong). There is no fixed size but most are about 40 centimeters in diameter with a rim lip of about 8 to 10 centimeters.

The gong is suspended from a handle by a cloth cord looped through two holes in the rim. To play, it is held in the performer's left hand and struck near the center with a large mallet, the tip of which is tightly wrapped in cloth. Its function is to reinforce the main beats of rhythmic patterns.

The *ching* was traditionally used in Korea for military signalling; it sounded retreat and a drum sounded advance. At present, it appears in ritual music performed in rites for royal ancestors (*see* Royal Ancestral Shrine Music in this chapter), in military processional music (*see* Processional Music in this chapter), in Shamanist and Buddhist rites, and in farmer's music (*see* Farmer's Music and Dance in this chapter).

Chin-go The largest Korean drum in current use, the *chin-go* is a barrel drum supported on a four-legged wooden stand. It has a painted red, slatted wooden body about 155 centimeters long with two cowhide heads about 110 centimeters in diameter tacked to each end. The head for striking has a multi-color decoration around the edge and a *yin-yang* symbol in the center. The player stands to perform and strikes the instrument with a soft-headed mallet.

The instrument, which is related to the Chinese *jingu,* came to Korea as part of a large gift of instruments sent to the Koryŏ court by the Sung Chinese emperor in 1116. Its use has always been limited to ceremonial music. Today it is only played in the music performed at rites for Confucius at Munmyo and rites for royal ancestors at Chongmyo (*see* Confucian Shrine Music and Royal Ancestral Shrine Music in this chapter). It is part of the ground orchestra, *hŏn-ga,* and is the counterpart of the smaller *chŏlgo* of the terrace orchestra, *tŭngga.* It functions chiefly as a punctuater of melodic phrases and also as part of the starting and stopping signals for the rest of the orchestra. Its sound can be very deep and imposing.

Chŏlgo The *chŏlgo* is a barrel drum mounted at a slant on a wooden stand. It has a painted red wooden body and a cowhide head is tacked to each end. The head for striking has a *yin-yang* symbol in the center and a multi-color decoration around the edge. The player sits in front of the drum and strikes the center of the head with a round-headed wooden mallet.

The instrument is considered of Chinese origin. It has always been restricted to ceremonial music. Today it is played only in the music performed in rites for Confucius at Munmyo and rites for royal ancestors at Chongmyo (*see* Confucian Shrine Music and Royal Ancestral Shrine Music in this chapter). It appears in the *tŭngga,* or terrace orchestra, and is the counterpart of the larger barrel drum *chin-go* that appears in the *hŏn-ga,* or ground orchestra. Its main function is to punctuate melodic phrases. It is also sounded as part of the starting and stopping signals for the ensemble.

Chŭk The *ch'uk,* or *kang* as it is also called, is a large percussion idiophone consisting of a wooden box and a round wooden hammer. The box, which is usually decorated with cloud and mountain motifs, is trapeziform with a large square top, a much smaller square bottom, and sloping sides. The top is about 55 centimeters square, the bottom about 43 centimeters square, and the height about 40 centimeters. The hammer protrudes from the top through a hole in the center.

For performance, the instrument is placed on a square wooden platform. To play, the performer lifts the hammer and pounds it solidly against the bottom of the box, producing a resounding thump.

The *ch'uk* functions solely as part of a starting signal. It plays three times after a stroke of the clappers, *pak* (*see* entry in this chapter). It is always paired with the wooden scraper, *ŏ* (*see* entry in this chapter), which gives the stopping signal.

The *ch'uk* has been used in ritual music in Korea ever since 1116 when the Sung Chinese emperor sent several as part of a large gift of musical instruments to the Koryŏ court. Presently it appears only in ensembles performing the ritual music at rites for Confucius and rites for royal ancestors (*see* Confucian Shrine Music and Royal Ancestral Shrine Music in this chapter).

Chwago The *chwago* is a medium size barrel drum with wooden body hung vertically in a wooden frame. The wooden body is painted with several bright colors and a cowhide head is tacked to each end. The heads have a *yin-yang* symbol in the center and a multi-color pattern around the edge.

The drum is hung in the frame with the heads vertical. The seated player strikes the drum on one head only with a large soft-headed wooden mallet. It produces a loud, deep sound with a long reverberation.

The instrument is thought to be a recent addition to Korean ensembles because it is not mentioned in early treatises or histories. Today it is used only in court and aristocratic music, especially in dance accompaniments. It provides support for the hourglass drum (*see Changgo*).

The name *chwago* literally means "seat drum" as *chwa* means "seat" and *go* means "drum."

Kkwaenggwari The *kkwaenggwari* is a small, lipped, flat bronze

gong that produces a remarkably loud, pene-
trating and clangorous sound. It is also
known by another onomatopoeic name,
kkaengmagi, and by the names *soe,* meaning "metal," and *sogŭm,* meaning "small
gong."

There are no fixed dimensions, but a
typical *kkwaenggwari* is about 20 centimeters in diameter and has a lip of
about 5 centimeters. The player supports
the instrument by putting his left thumb and fingers under the
upper lip. It is struck with a small wood or bamboo mallet with a
wooden ball at the end. The player can control the sound by
touching or not touching the gong surface with his fingers;
touching results in a damped sound, not touching in an open
sound.

Ancient records describe the *kkwaenggwari* in connection with
dances performed at the rites for royal ancestors (*see* Royal Ancestral Shrine Music in this chapter) and also indicate that it was
used to announce the beginning of the ritual performance.
Presently the instrument is used chiefly in farmer's music, *nong-
ak* (*see* Farmer's Music and Dance in this chapter). It is played by
the leader of the *nong-ak* band to signal rhythmic patterns to the
other musicians. The patterns played on the *kkwaenggwari* are
very rapid and complex. The *kkwaenggwari* is also used in
shamanistic music.

Mokt'ak The *mokt'ak* is a hand-held
wooden drum used only by
Buddhist monks to
accompany sutra chant-
ing (*see Yŏmbul*). It is
hollow and is shaped
like a slightly flattened
egg. It is carved from a
single piece of wood with a
handle at the apex and a slit around

the other end extending about halfway up either side. There is no standard size.

The player holds the instrument in his left hand and strikes it near the slit with a wooden mallet.

The name comes from *mok*, meaning "wood," and *t'ak*, meaning "bell."

Nodo The nodo consists of two small red barrel drums set atop each other at right angles on a long wooden pole that pierces their bodies. Knotted leather cords hang from each side of the drums. To play, the pole is twirled backward and forward so that the leather cords strike the drum heads, making a rustling sound.

The instrument is used in music performed in rites for Confucius and in rites for royal ancestors (*see* Confucian Shrine Music and Royal Ancestral Shrine Music in this chapter). It is played only as part of starting signals for the ground orchestra, *hŏn-ga*.

The *nodo* is considered Chinese. It began to be constructed in Korea in the fifteenth century based on descriptions from Chinese theoretical sources.

Nogo The *nogo* consists of two long red barrel drums set atop each other at right angles in a decorated two-pillar wooden frame. The pillars are mounted on two wooden stands, each consisting of four seated tigers. The top of the frame has a fire symbol in the center and a wooden dragon with long tassels hanging from its mouth at each end. For performance, the drums, only one head of each, are struck with a wooden mallet.

The instrument is used in music for Confucian rites and royal ancestral rites (*see* Confucian Shrine Music and Royal Ancestral Shrine Music in this chapter). It is played as part of the starting and stopping signals for the ground orchestra, *hŏn-ga*, and it is played for punctuation after every four notes of the slow melody.

The instrument is considered Chinese. It began to be made in Korea in the fifteenth century based on descriptions in Chinese theoretical sources.

Ŏ The ŏ is a wooden scraper in the shape of a tiger with a serrated backbone. It is about 100 centimeters long and 40 centimeters high and sits on a rectangular wooden platform about 40 centimeters high.

The instrument is played with a split bamboo whisk. The player strikes the head three times with the whisk and then drags it down the backbone. This is done three times as part of the signal for the music to halt. The sound that is produced does not come from the ŏ but from the bamboo whisk.

The instrument was first introduced to Korea from China in 1116 when the Sung Chinese emperor sent a large gift of musical instruments to the Koryŏ court. It now appears only in the ensembles that perform at the biannual rites for Confucius and the annual rites for royal ancestors (*see* Confucian Shrine Music and Royal Ancestral Shrine Music in this chapter). Its only musical function is to give the stopping signal. It is always paired with the *ch'uk* (pounded wooden box), which gives part of the starting signal.

Pak The *pak* is a fan-shaped clapper derived from the Chinese *paiban*. It consists of six wooden slabs about 40 centimeters long by 7 centimeters wide tied together loosely at one end with a cord made of deer skin. The slabs are thicker at the loose ends. To play, the slabs are spread and then pressed together suddenly resulting in a loud clap.

The instrument was used in Korea by 1078 when a number were received from China. More were received in 1116 when the Sung Chinese emperor sent a large gift of musical instruments to the Koryŏ court. Ancient records show it was a member of various court ensembles but was not used in ritual music.

It is now present in all large ensembles including ensembles for ritual music. It is played by the director of an ensemble to give a starting signal, one clap, and a stopping signal, three claps. It is also played in some *hyang-ak* and *tang-ak* pieces (*see* entries in this chapter) to mark off verses or rhythmic sections.

Pŏpko The *pŏpko* is a large barrel drum set aslant on a four-legged wooden stand. It is played by two players, one at each end of the drum and each using two wooden mallets. The players strike both the drumheads and the wooden body of the drum.

The name can be translated Buddhist drum; *pŏp* meaning "Buddhist," and *ko* meaning "drum."

Pu The *pu* is a large baked earthenware bowl played with a split bamboo brush. The bowl is placed on a square wooden stand. It is played by striking the rim of the bowl with the brush. The sound that is produced does not come from the bowl, but from the strips of bamboo striking the bowl and striking each other.

The instrument, which is thought to be a derivation of the Chinese *fou,* is now used only in performing ritual music in ceremonies honoring Confucius (*see* Confucian Shrine Music in this chapter). It is part of the ground orchestra, *hŏn-ga.* It plays an accelerated pattern after the melodic instruments have begun each note of the ritual music tune.

Puk The *puk* is a shallow double-headed barrel drum with a wooden body. It is an undecorated version of the *yonggo* (dragon drum) used in folk music. Its left head is struck with the palm of the left hand and its right head is struck with a stick held in the right hand.

Puk is also a generic term for drum.

P'yŏn-gyŏng The *p'yŏn-gyŏng* is a set of sixteen tuned L-shaped chimes. The chimes are made from a form of calcite which is white with a green hue. They are all about 40 to 45 centimeters long on the longer portion, about 30 centimeters long on the shorter portion, and about 6 centimeters wide on both. However, they vary in thickness from about 5.6 centimeters, the highest pitched chime, to 2.8 centimeters, the lowest pitched.

The chimes are hung in two rows of eight in an elaborately

decorated wooden frame. The frame, which is about 150 centimeters high and 190 centimeters long, is mounted on two stands, each consisting of a white wooden goose. Five wooden peacocks are along the top of the frame and a stylized phoenix head with long pheasant-feather tassels hanging from its mouth extend from each end. Each chime has a hole in it for suspending it from the frame. A number of *p'yŏn-gyŏng* were sent to Korea in 1116 as part of a gift of musical instruments from the Sung Chinese emperor. Koreans began manufacturing the instrument with native materials in the fifteenth century for use in court ceremonial and ritual music.

The instrument is still used in various pieces of music, most notably the ritual music performed at the biannual rites for Confucius and the annual rites for royal ancestors (*see* Confucian Shrine Music and Royal Ancestral Shrine Music in this chapter). It is always paired with the lower-pitched set of bronze bells *p'yŏnjong* (tuned bonze bells). The player sits behind the instrument and strikes one chime at a time with a mallet made of animal horn.

P'yŏnjong The *p'yŏnjong* is a set of sixteen tuned bronze bells. The bells are all basically the same shape and size, about 23 centimeters in height and 18 centimeters in diameter at the rim. However, the thickness of their walls is different, giving each one a different pitch.

The bells are hung in two rows of eight in a richly decorated wooden frame. The frame, which is about 150 centimeters high and 190 centimeters, is mounted on two stands, each consisting of four lions. Five wooden peacocks are along the top of the frame and a stylized dragon head with colored silk tassels hanging from its mouth extends from each end.

The instrument is used in the ritual music performed at the twice-yearly rites for Confucius and the annual rites for royal ancestors (*see* Confucian Shrine Music and Royal Ancestral Shrine Music in this chapter) and in several other pieces. It is always paired with the higher-pitched set of stone chimes *p'yŏngyŏng* (tuned L-shaped chimes). The player sits on the ground behind the instrument and strikes each bell on a slightly raised circle near the rim with a mallet made of animal horn.

The instrument, which is of Chinese origin, first came to Korea in 1116 as part of a gift of musical instruments sent to the Koryŏ court by the Sung Chinese emperor.

Sogo The *sogo*, or *maegubuk* as it is also known, is a small *(so)* double-headed shallow drum *(go)* with a wooden handle. It is about 30 centimeters in diameter and only a few centimeters thick. It has a wooden frame and two skins laced to each other. The frame is attached to a wooden handle.

The instrument is played with a thick wooden mallet but produces little sound. It is an important instrument in folk music, particularly farmer's band music and dance (*see* entry in this chapter). However, it functions more as a dance accoutrement than a musical instrument.

Yonggo The *yonggo*, or dragon drum as the name translates, is a shallow two-headed barrel drum. The heads are 35 to 40 centimeters in diameter and are made of tacked cowhide. The wooden body is about 20 to 25 centimeters deep and usually decorated with a brightly colored dragon *(yong)* motif. An undecorated version of the drum called *puk* is used in folk music.

The *yonggo* is now used in military processional music, *koch'wi*, and as an accompaniment for folk narrative singing, *p'ansori* (*see* entries in this chapter). In *koch'wi* it is hung skin upwards by a shoulder sash attached to two metal rings in the body of the drum and the player strikes it with two large wooden mallets. In *p'ansori* the player sits with the drum upright in front of him and strikes the head with the palm of his left hand and the barrel with a stick held in his right hand.

Pŏmp'ae, Ritual Chant

Considered the most important type of Buddhist chant, *pŏmp'ae*, or *pŏmŭn* as it is also called, is a solemn ritual chant performed only in association with certain rites. *Pŏmp'ae* texts are based on the Chinese language and Chinese poetic forms, but do not observe Chinese rhyme patterns. There are seven types of *pŏmp'ae* texts in Korea, each distinguished by the number of syllables and of text lines and all have extremely slow free rhythm. The meaning of the text is difficult to grasp because the melody of each syllable of text is greatly prolonged and because of the interpolation of certain vocables.

The *pŏmp'ae* repertory contains two different styles of chant: a short chant called *hossori*, and a long chant called *chissori*. It is used for short ceremonies. *Chissori* can be prolonged or abridged according to the requirements of the ceremony. It has a wide range of tone and makes use of falsetto singing.

Pŏmp'ae may be accompanied by a small hand-bell, a small wooden gong, or a large bronze gong.

Processional Music, *Koch'wi*

The music which was played for royal processions is called *koch'wi* in Korean and is often referred to in English as military music. It was performed by two bands: one at the front of the procession and one at the rear.

The front band, called *taech'wit'a* or *muryongchi gok*, preceded the king. It included *nabal* (long straight trumpet), *nagak* (conch shell horn), *t'aepyŏngso* (conical oboe), *chabara* (cymbals), *ching* (gong), *changgo* (hourglass drum) and *yonggo* (dragon drum) (*see* individual entries). The rear band, called *ch'wit'a* or *manp'a chongshik chi gok*, followed the king. It included *p'iri* (oboe), *sogŭm* (small transverse flute), *haegŭm* (spike fiddle), *changgo* and *chwago* (barrel drum) (*see* individual entries) and was not as loud as the front band. The snappy music of the front band heralded the

king and the quieter music of the rear band left onlookers with
an enhanced feeling of respect for their dignified leader.

Royal Ancestral Shrine Music, *Chongmyo-ak*

Chongmyo-ak is a term given to the music played during the
chehyang rites performed at the Chongmyo shrine to honor the
spirits of the Yi Dynasty kings and their queens (*see* Rites for Royalty in Beliefs and Customs; and Chongmyo Shrine in Famous
Places and Monuments). It is sometimes called *cherye-ak* and *a-
ak*.

Chinese ritual music was originally performed for the royal
ancestral rites. However, in the latter half of the fifteenth century,
King Sejo (r. 1455-68) ordered the music changed with the aim
of avoiding revering the spirits of the kings with music of Chinese origin. The music was thus arranged incorporating elements
of processional music, *koch'wi*, and Korean court music, *hyang-ak*
(*see* entries in this chapter) and some native Korean instruments.

Because the system of the Confucian rite was adopted for the
rites performed at the royal ancestral shrine, the organization of
the musicians is similar to that of the Confucian shrine music
(*see* entry in this chapter). The musicians are arranged in two
orchestras that perform antiphonally: the terrace, or *tŭngga*,
orchestra situated on the terrace of the shrine; and, the ground,
or *hŏn-ga*, orchestra situated in the courtyard. The music is
accompanied by ritual dances (*see* Confucian Dance in this chapter).

Salp'uri

Salp'uri is a highly expressive solo dance of spiritual cleansing.
The dancer's only prop is a long white scarf. As she dances, the
dancer goes through a series of emotions from sadness to invigo-
rating joy. The dancer expresses a wife's desire to call her dead

husband back to the world of the living, her ecstasy at meeting him, and her pain at reseparation.

Samulnori, Four-man Drumming and Dancing

The term *samulnori* means "the playing of four things." It was originally coined by a four-man drum and dance ensemble founded in 1978 who call themselves Samul Nori. The group combines traditional rhythmic constructs derived from the wandering bands of old (*see Kwangdae* in this chapter) with shamanistic ceremonies and modern compositions to create a unique musical experience that is both ancient and contemporary. The "four things" that are played are four percussion instruments: *changgo* (hourglass drum), *kkwaenggwari* (small gong), *puk* (barrel drum), and *ching* (large gong) (*see* individual entries in this chapter).

Because of the immense popularity of Samul Nori's music, similar performing groups have come into being and the word "*samulnori*" has become a generic term for the genre of music they perform.

Sanjo

Sanjo, literally meaning "scattered melodies," is an improvised solo instrumental form accompanied by *changgo* (hourglass drum). The *kayagŭm* (12-string long zither) is the traditional and most popular instrument for *sanjo*. However, other instruments, such as *kŏmun-go* (6-string long zither) and *taegŭm* (transverse flute), have been used for *sanjo* since the late nineteenth century.

A *sanjo* piece consists of six movements, each subdivided into several sections. The movements are played without a pause in progressively faster tempos. The movements have different tonal centers, rhythmic patterns and tempos.

The earliest *sanjo* music developed from the stringing together of shamanistic tunes and folk tunes from the Chŏlla region. These strung-together tunes became stock melodies for individual improvisation and elaboration and led to the creation of new melodies. The improvisational elements were given a formal structure with the imposition of a set framework of rhythms and modes. Because of the constraints of the modern stage, the improvisational techniques of *sanjo* have gradually disappeared and *sanjo* is even taught at the National Classical Music Institute of Korea.

Shamanic Music, *Shinawi*

Shinawi is the instrumental musical accompaniment for shamanistic ritual dances. The *shinawi* ensemble includes a *p'iri* (double-reed oboe), *taegŭm* (large transverse flute), *haegŭm* (spike fiddle), *changgo* (hourglass drum) or *puk* (double-headed barrel drum), *ching* (large gong), *para* (cymbals), and *kkwaenggwari* (small gong). The *p'iri*, *taegŭm*, and *haegŭm* are the main melodic instruments. The other instruments provide a variety of rhythmic patterns. Each player improvises independently of the others.

The basic musical elements of *shinawi* music are the same as those of two other genres, *p'ansori* and *sanjo* (*see* individual entries in this chapter), which are believed to have developed from *shinawi*.

Shijo

Shijo is a style of singing the three-line poetic form of the same name that was popular with the literati of the Chosŏn period (1392-1910) (*see* entry in Language and Letters). The poems are sung to a small number of standard melodies.

The standard accompaniment for the singer is *changgo* (hourglass drum). However, *p'iri* (double-reed oboe), *taegŭm* (large transverse flute) and *haegŭm* (two-string fiddle) are sometimes used in addition to *changgo*. The instrumental accompaniment is not prescribed; the instruments merely follow the vocal melody with ornaments and fill in the vocal pauses.

A *shijo* song contains two different rhythmic patterns—one five pulses and one eight pulses. Each note is given different types of vibrato, either upward or downward from the initiating pitch. The singer draws out the syllables of the text to such an extent that the meaning is lost unless one can actually see the poem.

Sŭngmu

One of the most expressive Korean folk dances is the solo dance *Sŭngmu*, the Monk's Dance. Inspired by Buddhist ritual dance, it is a blending of solemn movements and expressions with entertaining techniques. The dance, which involves a single framed drum, is done in a hooded robe with floor-length sleeves that was inspired by Buddhist robes.

The dancer, or "monk," vacillates between giving in to the call of the drum and scorning it. Tension mounts as he is successively drawn to the drum and repelled from it. Finally, incapable of resisting, he draws drumsticks out of his long sleeves and plays a spine-tingling solo on the drum. The tempo accelerates until the drummer gives up in exhaustion and leaves the stage with a dreamy look on his face and only the drum is left.

Some say the drum represents the ecstacy of enlightenment and some say it represents the temptation of worldly pleasures.

String Instruments

Ajaeng The *ajaeng* is a long bowed zither. It is made of paulownia wood and is about 160 centimeters long and 24 centimeters wide. It has seven strings of twisted silk and is bowed with a resined stick of forsythia wood about 65 centimeters long. The strings run from a gently curved bridge at the bowed end across seven small wooden movable bridges to another curved bridge at the other end. The instrument is played propped up at the bowing end, the performer's right, on a small four-legged stand. The performer bows with his right hand and presses down on the strings with his left hand a few centimeters left of the movable bridges.

A smaller version of the instrument, the *sanjo ajaeng,* was invented in the 1960s. It is similar to the older version in most ways but it is shorter, about 120 centimeters, and has eight strings. Instead of a separate wooden stand, it has a flap of wood hinged to the bottom that unfolds to form a prop.

The *ajaeng* came to Korea from China during the Koryŏ period (918-1392). It was used only in Chinese music but was later adopted for use in Korean native music. It now appears in both court and folk ensembles and is usually paired with another bowed string instrument, the *haegŭm.* Since the invention of the *sanjo ajaeng,* the instrument has become increasingly popular in

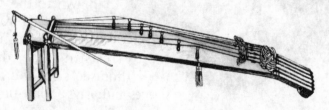

the virtuoso solo genre *sanjo* (*see* entry in this chapter).

Haegŭm The *haegŭm* is a two-string spike fiddle known ono-matopoeically as *kkangkkang-i*. It is about 70 centimeters long. The neck, which is made of bamboo or wood and is about 2.5 centimeters in diameter, curves slightly forward at the top and passes through a tubular soundbox at the bottom. The soundbox is made of large bamboo root or hardwood about 10 centimeters in length and diameter and has a paulownia wood sound-table at the front and is open at the rear. Two strings of twisted silk are strung from a metal clasp at the bottom of the soundbox, across a small movable wooden bridge on the front of the soundbox and tied to two large pegs skewered into the curved portion of the neck. The pegs are about 11 centimeters long and have spools on which excess string is wound. The bow, which is about 65 centimeters long, is made of slender supple bamboo and strung with horsehair.

The instrument is held on the left knee and played vertically with the bow inserted horizontally between the strings. The player alters the tension of the horsehair by pushing down on it with the fingers of the bowing hand. The fingers of the left hand pull the strings toward the neck. The instrument has a nasal timbre which is distinctive enough to be heard in large ensembles.

The *haegŭm* is believed to be of Mongolian origin. It was used only in Korean native music *hyang-ak* (*see* entry in this chapter) until the end of the fifteenth century but it is now used for Chinese music *tang-ak* (*see* entry in this chapter). It is usually played in mixed ensembles. It is a favorite instrument in shamanistic ensembles (*shinawi*) and folk song accompaniments and it sometimes serves as soloist in *sanjo* (*see* entry in this chapter).

The name of the instrument comes from *hae*, the name of a Tartar tribe, and *gŭm*, meaning "string instrument."

Kayagŭm Koreans' favorite instrument, the *kayagŭm*, or *kayatgo* as it is often called, is a long twelve-string zither with a very long history. It can be traced back to the Shilla Kingdom when,

according to the
Samguk sagi (*History
of the Three King-
doms; see* entry in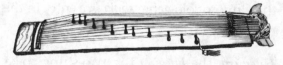
Language and Letters), it was invented in the sixth century by
King Kashil of Kaya, a tribal league in the southern part of the
Korean peninsula.

Today there are two kinds: the *chŏng-ak kayagŭm,* which is
used for court and aristocratic music, and the *sanjo kayagŭm,*
which is used for folk and virtuoso music. The *chŏng-ak kayagŭm,*
which is also called *pŏpkŭm* and *p'ungnyu kayagŭm,* is about 160
centimeters long and 30 centimeters wide. It is fashioned from a
single piece of paulownia wood with a curving front and partially hollowed out back. At the lower end stylized ram's horns are
carved out of the board. It has twelve strings of twisted silk that
run from pegs at the top end, through small holes, over a curved
fixed bridge, across twelve movable bridges about 6 to 7 centimeters high, and across a fixed bridge to looped moorings where
reserve string is coiled.

The *sanjo kayagŭm* is about 142 centimeters long and 23 centimeters wide. It resembles the *chŏng-ak kayagŭm* in most ways,
but the body is not made of one piece of wood but of two, the
front of paulownia wood and the back of chestnut wood; the
curvature of the front is more pronounced; there is only a hint
of the ram's horns; and, there is no lower fixed bridge.

To play, the top end of the instrument is supported on the performer's right knee with the lower end pointing slightly away
from the performer's left so that it passes in front of the left knee.
The performer plucks and flicks the strings with the fleshy part
of the fingers of the right hand while pressing down on the
strings with the fingers of the left hand, a few centimeters to the
left of the movable bridges.

Kŏmun-go The *kŏmun-go* is a long six-string zither which was
invented in the fourth century by a Korean musician of Koguryŏ
named Wang San-ak. The name comes from *kŏmun,* meaning
"black," and *go,* meaning "zither."

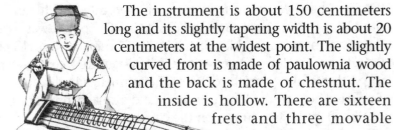

The instrument is about 150 centimeters long and its slightly tapering width is about 20 centimeters at the widest point. The slightly curved front is made of paulownia wood and the back is made of chestnut. The inside is hollow. There are sixteen frets and three movable bridges. The strings of twisted silk run from a broad, curved bridge at the top end of the instrument to looped moorings at the bottom end where reserve string is coiled. The first, fifth and sixth strings are stretched over the bridges and the second, third and fourth strings are stretched over the frets.

The instrument is played propped slightly up on edge and angled away from the performer so that the bottom lies against his left knee and the outer edge of the right end is supported above his right knee. The player plucks the strings both downward and upward with a pencil-size bamboo stick *(sultae)* held between the index finger and middle finger of the right hand while the fingers of the left hand press on the strings to produce microtones.

Fretted instruments resembling *kŏmun-go* appear in tomb paintings of the Koguryŏ period (37 B.C.-A.D. 668). The *kŏmun-go* was a major instrument during the Three Kingdoms period (57 B.C.-A.D. 935). Today it is used in many court and folk ensembles and in the solo virtuoso genre *sanjo* (*see* entry in this chapter).

Pip'a A pear-shaped, short-necked plucked lute which is no longer used, the *pip'a* was introduced to Korea from Central Asia through northern China in the Three Kingdoms period (57 B.C.-A.D. 668). It was one of the major string instruments during the Unified Shilla period (668-935).

There were two kinds of *pip'a*: the *hyang pip'a*, used for native Korean music, and the *tang pip'a*, used for Chinese secular music.

Wolgŭm The *wolgŭm* is a four-string plucked lute which can be traced back to the Koguryŏ period (37 B.C.-A.D. 668). It was used in Korean music ensembles in the early Chosŏn period (1392-1910) but is no longer used today. It is about 104 centimeters long with a round soundbox about 37 centimeters in diameter. It has twelve frets on the long thin neck and a small thirteenth fret positioned under two strings on the circular sound table.

The name *wolgŭm* literally means "moon zither."

Yanggŭm The *yanggŭm* is the only traditional instrument with strings made of steel wire instead of silk. It is trapeziform and measures about 71 centimeters on the longest side, 47 centimeters on the parallel side, and 28 centimeters on the two shortest sides. It has fourteen sets of four metal strings which pass over and under two bridges. The strings are struck with a thin bamboo stick to play.

The *yanggŭm* is the Korean counterpart of the Persian *santur* and its name literally translates as "foreign zither." The instrument, which was adapted for Korean music ensembles, is believed to have been introduced to Korea in the eighteenth century by Korean envoys to China where it had been introduced by Christian missionaries around the sixteenth century. It is now used only in mixed ensembles for aristocratic music. Unlike most other Korean melodic instruments, it is incapable of vibrato or pitch shading.

Wind Instruments

Chi The *chi* is a short transverse bamboo flute with a mouthpiece. It has five finger-holes, the first one displaced to the side.

The far end of the tube is blocked except for a cross-shaped hole which may be stopped with the side of the little finger of the player's right hand to produce certain pitches and semi-tones. The raised notched mouthpiece is made of bamboo. It is mounted on the tube with wax.

The *chi* is considered a purely Chinese instrument. It is used only in the ritual music performed in the rites for Confucius (*see* Confucian Shrine Music in this chapter) and in concert performances of the ritual music.

Hun The *hun* is a globular vessel flute related to the Chinese *xun*. It is made of clay and is shaped like two-thirds of an egg. It has a blowing-hole at the apex, three finger-holes on the front, and two thumb-holes on the back. There is no fixed size but the instrument is small enough to fit into cupped hands.

The *hun* is required to produce twelve chromatic notes of a single octave. Because *hun* is made of baked clay, the tuning is unpredictable. Therefore, a great many are usually made at one time and the correctly tuned ones selected.

Hun were introduced to Korea from China when the Sung Chinese emperor sent a large gift of musical instruments to the Koryŏ Kingdom in 1114 and 1116. *Hun* were first made in Korea during the reign of King Sejong (r. 1418-50), who did much to improve music and musical instruments (*see* entry in Historic Figures).

Today the *hun* is considered purely Chinese and is used only in the musical ensembles at the twice-yearly rites for Confucius held in Seoul (*see* Confucian Shrine Music in this chapter).

Nabal The *nabal* is a long brass trumpet similar to the Chinese *laba*. It has no finger-holes. It is now played exclusively for military processional music (*see* entry in this chapter) to produce only a single pitch, alternating long-sustained notes with the *nagak,* a conch shell trumpet.

The *nabal* is the only Korean wind instrument made of metal. Its long tube can be broken into two or three segments for storage.

Nagak The *nagak* is a conch shell horn, and the name means just that; *na* is conch and *gak* is horn. It is also called *na* and *sora,* other names for conch. Construction of the horn involves merely fashioning a mouthpiece at the narrow end of the shell.

The horn produces a single deep pitch. The timbre is warm and hornlike but not brassy.

The instrument was played in royal processions as early as the Koryŏ period (918-1392). During the Chosŏn period (1392-1910), it was used primarily in military processional bands. *Akhak kwebŏm,* a 1493 treatise on music, noted it as part of the dance paraphernalia used in performances during the rites for royal ancestors (*see* Royal Ancestral Shrine Music in this chapter).

At present it is used exclusively in ensembles for military processional music (*see* entry in this chapter). It alternates long-held notes with the trumpet, *nabal.*

P'iri The *p'iri* is a cylindrically bored double reed oboe-like instrument made of bamboo. It has seven finger-holes and a thumbhole. The mouthpiece is longer and wider than that of the Western oboe.

There are three types of *p'iri*: *hyang p'iri, se p'iri,* and *tang p'iri.* The *hyang p'iri* is the largest at about 27 centimeters long. It has a shaved bamboo double reed which is 7 centimeters long and 1 centimeter wide. It has a distinctive loud, rough nasal timbre. It is always the lead instrument in ensembles and it appears in both court music and folk music. The *se p'iri* is about 23 centimeters long and has a smaller bore and softer, gentler tone than the *hyang p'iri.* Because of its soft tone, it is not found in large orchestras but in ensembles which accompany singing or in ensembles of soft string instruments. The *tang p'iri* is about the same length as the *se p'iri* but it is much thicker and has a larger bore. Its tone is even more strident than the *hyang p'iri* and it is used only for court music.

So The *so* is a set of panpipes consisting of sixteen notched bamboo pipes fitted into a thin symmetrical wooden frame. Because it is shaped like the wings of a bird, it is also known as *pongso*, which literally means "phoenix pipes," *pong* meaning "phoenix" and *so* meaning "pipes."

The pipes are closed at the bottom. Tuning is done by partially filling the tubes with wax to adjust the length of the air columns. The player holds the *so* in both hands by the thin edges of the frame and blows into the pipes to produce long equally spaced notes of about 4 seconds each.

So were included in large gifts of musical instruments the Koryŏ court received from Sung China in 1114 and 1116. However, fourth century tomb paintings show that they were in use in Korea long before then.

The *so* is now considered purely Chinese and used solely in the ritual music performed to honor Confucius (*see* Confucian Shrine Music in this chapter).

Sogŭm The *sogŭm*, which is also called *tangjŏk*, is a small transverse bamboo flute similar to the Western piccolo. It has a mouth-hole and six finger-holes. It is no longer played.

Taegŭm The *taegŭm*, or *chŏttae* as it is called in pure Korean, is a large transverse bamboo flute about 80 centimeters long. In the

name, *tae* means "large," and *gǔm* means "flute." The instrument has six finger-holes plus a blowing-hole and a membrane-covered hole. It has a relatively large mouth-hole which allows a gradation of pitches to be produced. Between the mouth-hole and the first finger-hole is an aperture covered with a thin membrane of river reed that produces a buzzing sound which distinguishes the *taegǔm* from other flutes.

Because of its size, the instrument is awkward to play. The performer must support the extension of the blowing-hole end on his left shoulder and bend his left wrist sharply backward to reach the finger-holes.

The *taegǔm* has been a dominant instrument in Korea since the Unified Shilla period (668-935). It is used in both court music and folk music. It is used as a tuning instrument in ensembles.

Taep'yǒngso The *taep'yǒngso* is a double-reed instrument with seven finger-holes on the front and a thumb-hole on the back. It is made of hardwood, has a broad conical bore, and uses a short, narrow double reed. It is about 47 cen-
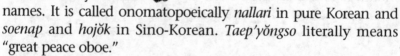
timeters long with a small circular metal lip disk below the reed and a large cup-shaped metal bell at the lower end.

The *taep'yǒngso* is referred to by several names. It is called onomatopoeically *nallari* in pure Korean and *soenap* and *hojǒk* in Sino-Korean. *Taep'yǒngso* literally means "great peace oboe."

The *taep'yǒngso* is believed to have been introduced from China about the turn of the fifteenth century. It was used for military processional music and other court functions during the

Chosŏn period (1392-1910) but it is now used for royal ancestral shrine music, farmer's band music in which it is the only melodic instrument, and traditional military music (*see* Royal Ancestral Shrine Music; Farmer's Music and Dance; and Processional Music in this chapter). Its loud piercing sound is well suited to outdoor performances.

Tanso The *tanso* is a small, end-blown bamboo notched flute about 40 centimeters long. It has four finger-holes on the front and a thumb-hole on the back.

It is primarily played in chamber music ensembles and is a favorite solo instrument because of its exceedingly pure and delicate tone.

The name comes from *tan,* meaning "short," and *so,* meaning "pipe."

Yŏmbul, Sutra Recitation

Yŏmbul, meaning "invocation," is musically the simplest of the Buddhist ritual chants. It is the recitation of sutra to the accompaniment of a wooden gong called *mokt'ak* (*see* entry). The sutras include texts translated into Chinese from Sanskrit, in which the meaning of the sutra can be conveyed, and texts written in Sanskrit or transliterated into Chinese from Sanskrit, in which one must understand Sanskrit to grasp the meaning.

LANGUAGE AND LETTERS

Han-gŭl, Korean Alphabet

The Korean alphabet, called *han-gŭl,* consists of twenty-four letters, fourteen consonants and ten vowels. The letters are combined to form phonemes so that the actual number of letters is increased to forty, nineteen consonants and twenty-one vowels.

Han-gŭl is a true alphabet but it incorporates the characteristics of a syllabary; that is, letters are always arranged in syllable blocks. This makes it possible to write Korean from top to bottom or from right to left, without having to turn the letters around in any way. Another advantage is that *han-gŭl* and Chinese characters, which are commonly used in Korea, can be readily mixed in writing and printing.

Han-gŭl, or *ka-na-da* as the alphabet is often called using its first three syllables, is one of the most scientific phonetic alphabets in existence. The phonemic symbols are derived from the shape or form of the organs of speech (i.e. the mouth, the tongue, the throat) and the shape the organs take during articulation.

Instead of evolving, the alphabet was consciously created by a group of scholars King Sejong (*see* entry in Historic Figures) commissioned in 1443 to develop a script which would enable Koreans of all classes to express themselves in writing in their own language—a Ural-Altaic language whose origin is lost in antiquity. Until the invention of *han-gŭl,* Koreans used Chinese characters to express themselves in writing; sometimes using the characters to represent their original meaning and sometimes simply to represent sounds *(see* Writing System in this chapter).

The alphabet the scholars invented consisted of twenty-eight letters, seventeen consonants and eleven vowels, but with time three consonants and one vowel dropped out of use. It was promulgated under the name *hunmin chŏng-ŭm,* meaning "correct sounds for teaching the people," by King Sejong in October 1446. However, the literati were opposed to using it and most continued to write in classical Chinese. It was generally called *ŏnmun,* or vulgar script, until the latter years of the nineteenth century when it gained prestige in the wake of increasing national pride and was redesignated *kungmun,* or national script. *Kungmun* was later rejected because the term itself is a Chinese compound. The term *han-gŭl,* meaning "Korean writing," has been used since the early twentieth century.

Hyangga

Hyangga is the term for the poetry of the Shilla (57 B.C.-A.D.935) and early Koryŏ (918-1932) periods written in Korean by means of the *idu* or *hyangch'al* script *(see* Writing System in this chapter). *Hyangga* vary in length from four to eight or ten lines.

Only twenty-five *hyangga* survive. Most of them reflect strong Buddhist tendencies and deal with the mysteries of life and death.

The word *hyangga* is also loosely used as a generic term to encompass all the Korean language lyric forms of the Three Kingdoms and early Koryŏ periods to set them apart from the Chinese language poetic forms that existed at the time.

Kasa

Kasa is a long descriptive, and often episodic, narrative in poetic form characterized by extended use of grammatical parallelism. It emerged during the final years of the Koryŏ period (918-1392) and the initial years of the Chosŏn period (1392-1910). It became a favorite of the Confucian scholar and reached its zenith in the late sixteenth century.

A favorite theme of kasa writers was the charm and pleasures of a rustic life which was often expressed using a seasonal framework. Other popular themes included the sorrow of unrequited love, the hardship of exile, the pleasures of the farmer's life, the beauties of nature, pledges of loyalty to the sovereign, and the joys of a life of retirement. Women of the upper classes used kasa to express the sorrow of their restrained life.

Samguk sagi, History of the Three Kingdoms

The oldest extant Korean history, Samguk sagi (History of the Three Kingdoms) was compiled in 1145 by a high government official named Kim Pu-shik by order of Injong (r. 1122-46), the seventeenth ruler of the Koryŏ Kingdom. It was written on the basis of native Korean sources, which no longer exist, and with reference to Chinese histories. It was written in annals form with separate biographies, treatises, and chronological tables.

Samguk sagi was compiled from an aristocratic point of view and a Confucianist historiographical perspective, that is, one may learn from history by studying the virtues and vices of past rulers. An effort was made to humanize the legends and myths of the past and interpret them as distortions of events that actually occurred in order to fit them into a Confucian framework of attitudes.

Samguk yusa, Memorabilia of the Three Kingdoms

Samguk yusa (Memorabilia of the Three Kingdoms) is a collection of Buddhist lore that is usually classed as a history because of its immeasurable importance to Korean historiography. It was written in the late thirteenth century by a Buddhist monk named Iryŏn (*see* Historic Figures), but it was not printed until 1512. It was intended to complement *Samguk sagi (History of the Three Kingdoms; see* entry in this chapter) which was written in 1145.

The title is a misnomer as the book deals mainly with the Shilla Kingdom and also goes far beyond the Three Kingdoms into the Koryŏ Kingdom of Iryŏn's day. It is not a systematic work, having been a product of Iryŏn's leisure activities. Nonetheless, it includes names and dates and references to some source materials, including *Samguk sagi,* which still exists. It is especially valuable because it provides much insight into the beliefs, practices and everyday life of the people of thirteenth century Korea.

The book contains legends and tales related to the founding and early history of the three kingdoms of Koguryŏ, Paekche and Shilla. It also includes stories about the establishment of Buddhism, mostly in Shilla, and stories about the lives and miracles of famous Buddhist monks and about filial piety.

A unique feature of *Samguk yusa* is that it begins Korean history with the man-god Tan-gun (*see* entry in Historic Figures). At the time it was written, the Korean people were suffering under Mongol dominion, so perhaps Iryŏn wished to give his people a sense of identity as a superior race with a common ancestor who descended directly from heaven.

Shijo

Shijo is a traditional poetic form of three lines, each line made up of four rhythmic groupings with a minor pause at the end of the second line and a major pause at the end of the fourth. The first line introduces a theme, the second develops it, and the third draws the conclusion to the poem. There is often a deliberate twist in phrasing or meaning in the third line. The interplay of sound, rhythm and meaning is the essence of the *shijo* and the basis of its structure.

Shijo came into being during the Koryŏ period (918-1392) and further developed during the Chosŏn period (1392-1910) to become a major genre of native literature. It became a necessary component of the education of every upper-class gentlemen. *Shijo* were sung and orally transmitted until the texts began to be written down from the eighteenth century onward.

The themes range from court and country, friendship and love, praise and satire to time and change. There are *shijo* that inculcate moral precepts, express loyalty to the sovereign, sing of the valiant spirit of the soldier, extol the beauties of nature, depict the bitterness of the downtrodden, sing of Confucian virtues, give voice to a yearning, and sing the joys of rusticity.

The *shijo* is Korea's most traditional poetic form and *shijo* are still composed today.

Writing System

In writing, Koreans use both the Korean alphabet *han-gŭl* (*see* entry in this chapter) and Chinese characters, which are called *hanja* in Korean. Chinese characters are usually mixed with Korean for the sake of brevity and clarification. A knowledge of eighteen hundred Chinese characters, which are taught in middle school and high school, is necessary to read basic textbooks, newspapers and magazines. Of course, to become an expert in a particular field requires an even broader knowledge of Chinese characters. The ability to use Chinese characters proficiently is considered prestigious as it is indicative of a strong and advanced education.

Although Korean and Chinese are very different languages, Koreans have used Chinese characters for writing since ancient times. The Chinese writing system probably came to Korea about the fourth century B.C. but did not come into widespread use until the second or third century A.D.

Using the Chinese writing system entailed many disadvantages, so a method of representing a Korean word with a Chinese character having its sound or with one sharing its meaning was developed along with a set of rules for its use. At first, Chinese characters were arranged in Korean word order but later a system called *idu* was devised to put a sentence into Korean syntax. With time a more sophisticated system called *hyangch'al* came into use. It expressed Korean nouns with Chinese characters having the same meaning and grammatical elements, verb stems and inflections with arbitrary Chinese characters having the desired pronunciation.

These clumsy systems of writing were used until *han-gŭl* was invented in the fifteenth century. *Han-gŭl* made all Korean sounds easily recordable and facilitated learning the correct Korean pronunciation of Chinese characters.

There are two ways to write in Korean: from top to bottom, and from left to right. From top to bottom is the more traditional way of writing. It is done from top to bottom, starting at the right side of the page and moving to the left.

HISTORIC FIGURES

An Chung-gŭn

One of Korea's greatest heroes of modern times, An Chung-gŭn (1879-1910) was an independence fighter who assassinated Ito Hirobumi, the mastermind of Japan's annexation of Korea.

The eldest son of a wealthy, scholarly family of Haeju, Hwang-hae-do Province (now in North Korea), An was highly knowledgeable of the Chinese classics and excelled in calligraphy. He grew up at a time when Japan, China, Russia, Britain, France, and the United States were vying for dominance over Korea and factionalism was rife within the royal court, due in part to young scholars who, having been exposed to Western ideas via China and Japan, called for modernization to ensure national survival and saw education as the first step toward that goal.

In 1905, Japan sent its elder statesman Ito Hirobumi to Seoul to conclude a protectorate treaty. He entered the palace with an escort of Japanese troops, demanded King Kojong and his ministers accept the treaty, and, when they refused, ordered Japanese soldiers to bring the official seal from Korea's foreign ministry and affix it to the treaty. This act of aggression completely deprived Korea of the sovereign power to maintain relations with foreign governments and provided for the appointment of a Japanese resident-general to a position directly under the Korean monarch to take charge of Korea's foreign relations. Shortly thereafter, An went to Shanghai, China in the hope of finding a man among the Koreans there who could lead a united struggle to combat Japan's domination of Korea.

However, he soon returned home upon receiving word that his father had died and with his inheritance set up several schools to educate young people to work for Korean independence. As the national situation worsened, he turned his schools over to others and took up arms to fight the Japanese. In the autumn of 1907 he went to Vladisvostok where many Korean independence fighters were living in exile and organized a fighting group called the Korean Righteous Army and became its deputy chief of staff. The force attacked Japanese troops in forays across the Tumen River.

In the spring of 1909 An and a dozen of the fighters left the army to wage their own battles. Each of them cut off the tip of their left ring finger and wrote his name in blood on the Korean flag. An vowed to the other members of the Society of Cut Fingers, as they called themselves, that he would kill Ito Hirobumi.

On October 26, 1909, in the Harbin railroad station, An shot Ito just minutes after he disembarked from a train and, confirming that he had fallen, shouted "Long live Korean independence!"

He was arrested on the spot and subsequently brought to trial before a Japanese court in Port Arthur. He proudly told the court that the killing of Ito was only part of the Korean war for independence and that he killed him for the independence of the nation as well as for peace in the Orient. The court sentenced him to death on February 14, 1910 and he was executed in the Japanese prison in Port Arthur on March 26. While in prison awaiting his execution, he wrote many poems and articles including an autobiography.

An's noble actions and personal sacrifice elevated the spirit of the Korean people and shocked the Japanese by bringing their crimes and atrocities to the attention of the world.

Chinul

One of the greatest figures in the history of Korean Buddhism, Chinul (1158-1210), or National Preceptor Pojo as he is also known, established the basic outlook of the form of Korean Sŏn (Zen) Buddhism called Chogye-jong. His writings and teachings are a central part of the present monastic study program and his instructions for meditation are followed in most Sŏn monasteries in Korea.

Chinul was born at a time when Koryŏ was experiencing political upheaval and religious deterioration. He entered a monastery at age seven and became a monk at age fifteen. He passed the clerical examinations for pursuing a career in the monastic hierarchy before age twenty-five. However, because of the degeneration of the institutionalized religion that was becoming increasingly worldly and conflicts between the two streams of Koryŏ Buddhism, Sŏn (meditative) and Kyo (doctrinal), he retreated into the mountains to devote himself to study and contemplation.

In 1185 he had a religious experience that convinced him of the similarity of the aims of the Sŏn and the Kyo sects and vowed to work to unite the two. In 1190, he founded a community at Kŏjosa Temple with several like-minded friends to pursue a pure religious life. For the next seven years they remained there, their number steadily increasing as more and more monks were attracted to their practice of Buddhism. In 1200 Chinul went to Chogyesan Mountain where some of his followers were enlarging a hermitage into a monastery. The work took five years to complete and the temple became known as Songgwangsa.

Chinul remained at Songgwangsa until his death, working for the revitalization of Buddhist spiritual life and the unification of the various Buddhist orders into a single, cooperative community. He taught extensively, led retreats, and wrote many works on Buddhist philosophy and monastic practice. His fame spread and he finally gained the respect of the court which he had initially shunned. He died in 1210 while sitting on his lecture seat discussing points of doctrine with his disciples. He was given the posthumous title National Preceptor Pojo.

Chinul taught that once one achieves sudden elightenment, that is, becomes awakened to the fact that the human mind is none other than the Buddha-mind, the mind must be constantly cultivated. He emphasized constant discipline, prayer, sutra study and meditation.

Chŏng Mong-ju

A symbol of fidelity and unswerving loyalty, Chŏng Mong-ju (1337-92) was one of the most influential figures of his time. He was born when the Koryŏ Kingdom was devastated, spiritless and on the brink of collapse following fifty years of Mongol domination that was preceded by forty years of bloody resistance. Like many other young scholars, he turned to the Neo-Confucian philosophy of Chu Hsi, or Chujahak as it is called in Korean.

Chong was a highly versatile scholar and statesman. He was sent several times on special diplomatic missions to Japan and to China where he won great respect and improved relations between Koryŏ and the Ming court. However, he was primarily concerned with the promotion of Confucian education and the creation of a corps of leaders of high moral integrity and fortitude. He was instrumental in a movement to establish Confucian academies and shrines in major provincial towns and cities and helped found five Confucian academies, which were collectively called *obu haktang,* in the five wards of the capital.

He supported his great friend Yi Sŏng-gye (*see* entry in this chapter) when he implemented a sweeping land reform. However, because Confucian tradition made no allowance for a switch of loyalty to another sovereign by revolt, he refused to accept the advent of a new dynasty proposed by Yi. Subsequently, he was assassinated by Yi's fifth son, Yi Pang-won (1367-1422), who later ruled from 1400 to 1418 and is known to history by the dynastic name T'aejong.

Iryŏn

The author of *Samguk yusa (Memorabilia of the Three Kingdoms; see* entry in Language and Letters), an ancient book of immeasurable importance to Korean historiography, Iryon was born Kim Kyŏn-myŏng in 1206 in Kyŏngsan, an area not far from Kyŏngju. He entered a Buddhist order at an early age and was given the Buddhist name Iryŏn. At age twenty-two, he passed the national examination for Sŏn (Zen) monks with the highest distinction and thereafter devoted himself to teaching and studying at various temples. He died in 1289 at age eighty-three.

He was instrumental in popularizing Sŏn, the contemplative school of Buddhism, and wrote over a hundred books on Sŏn

Buddhism, though only a list of their titles remains.

Ironically, it is not for his contribution to the development of Buddhism that he is remembered but for his contribution to Korean historiography in the form of *Samguk yusa*. Perhaps more importantly, by beginning *Samguk yusa* with the story of Tan-gun, the man-god who founded the Korean nation (*see* entry in this chapter), he fostered national pride by strengthening the people's sense of identity as a distinct race and giving force to the concept that they were descended from a common ancestor. He showed great respect for the legacies and traditions of the past and his work is all the more valuable because it records life, beliefs, and practices of the thirteenth century.

Kim Ch'un-ch'u

Kim Ch'un-ch'u (?-661), or T'aejong Muyŏl as he is known by his dynastic title, was the twenty-ninth ruler of Shilla. The grandson of Shilla's King Chinji-wang (r. 576-579), he was a brilliant diplomat and the mastermind behind Shilla's unification of the Korean Peninsula.

At the time Kim began to work his wonders, Shilla was not in a very good position to attempt to unify the peninsula. The kingdom was wedged into the southeast corner of the peninsula by the powerful Koguryŏ Kingdom in the north, and by the Paekche Kingdom in the west. Moreover, it was at odds with the Japanese across the sea who were looking for an opportunity to attack and the Chinese who ambitiously wanted to bring the Korean Peninsula under their control.

Aware of the need to placate Japan, which maintained a close relationship with Paekche, Kim went to Japan for a year in 647 and managed to improve relations somewhat. He then visited China twice and eventually persuaded the T'ang court to enter into a military alliance.

When Queen Chindŏk-yŏwang (r. 647-654) died in 654, Kim ascended the Shilla throne and set in motion a plan to conquer Paekche and Koguryŏ. His strategy was to attack the weaker

Paekche first to isolate the more formidable Koguryŏ and to stall a Japanese approach to Paekche and then subdue Koguryŏ. In 660, Kim stormed into Paekche in a pincers movement with 130,000 Chinese soldiers commanded by Chinese General Su Ting-fang and 50,000 Shilla soldiers commanded by General Kim Yu-shin, Kim's brother-in-law. Paekche, whose military power had been needlessly wasted on earlier attacks on Shilla, capitulated after putting up little resistance.

The fall of Paekche placed Koguryŏ, which was rent by internal power struggles and whose military and economic resources were exhausted after years of war with China, in a strategically dangerous situation. However, Kim Ch'un-ch'u was not to see the day the peninsula was finally unified under Shilla. He died in 661, leaving the task to be completed by his son, King Munmu-wang (r. 661-681), who defeated Koguryŏ in 668 through a coordinated Shilla and T'ang offensive launched in 667 and eventually repulsed the T'ang forces by force of arms, thereby preserving the independence of the Korean Peninsula.

Kim Yu-shin

One of Korea's greatest heroes, Kim Yu-shin (595-673) was an outstanding warrior and resourceful military strategist who helped make Shilla the dominant military power on the Korean Peninsula in the seventh century. Even in his own day, he was the greatest hero of the unification wars, being chiefly responsible for the victories that led to the unification of the peninsula under Shilla. He was instrumental in helping his brother-in-law Prince Kim Ch'un-ch'u (*see* entry in this chapter) ascend to the throne and plan the conquest of Paekche and Koguryŏ.

Growing up at a time when Shilla was perpetually entangled in territorial disputes with the neighboring kingdoms of Koguryŏ and Paekche, Kim dreamed of unifying the three kingdoms from an early age. At the age of fifteen, he joined the *hwarang* (*see* entry in Miscellaneous), a band of patriotic youths who in times of peace led a life of pilgrimage and prayer for the prosperity of the nation and in times of war spearheaded the fighting.

In 629, when the morale of his soldiers plummeted during an attack on Koguryŏ, Kim rode at the head of a suicide squad and in one swift movement beheaded the enemy general. The battle was the first of a long series of victorious campaigns he led.

Kim's victories were the result of his resourcefulness in military strategies as well as his expertise in psychological warfare and counterintelligence. Well aware that T'ang China, with whom Shilla had a military alliance, was intent on annexing the Korean Peninsula, he staged a meeting where he advocated very loud and clear for a war with T'ang China, knowing full well that his words would be reported to the T'ang army by an informant. As he expected, the meeting was reported and the T'ang army, recognizing Shilla's fierce determination to defend itself, withdrew from Shilla.

Kim died in 673 at age seventy-nine. Though he had succeeded in conquering Paekche and Koguryŏ, the T'ang forces were yet to be driven from the land. Nonetheless, he died convinced that Shilla would triumph over them and, just several days before his death, he even gave King Munmu-wang (r. 661-681) advice on what to do when peace was achieved. He was posthumously given the title Hŭngmu-taewang, meaning "Great King Hŭngmu."

Sejong the Great

The most revered of all Korean kings is Sejong Taewang, the fourth king of Chosŏn who ruled from 1418 to 1450. Koreans regard him as Korea's wisest and most gifted ruler primarily for his invention of the Korean alphabet *han-gŭl* (*see* entry in Language and Letters), which gave Koreans of all classes an alphabet with which to express themselves in writing in their own language.

However, it is for much more than the invention of the alphabet that Sejong is called the Great (*Taewang*) and his 32-year reign is recognized as the most brilliant and fructuous in

Chosŏn's 518 years.

One of his greatest achievements, and one which led to many of the others, was the establishment of the Hall of Worthies (Chiphyŏnjŏn), an institute for the accumulation and dissemination of knowledge useful in government and to the populace. Some of the finest intellects of the day were gathered in the center, which, in reality, was the reorganization of an older institute of the same name which had become so ineffective that it existed in name only.

Much of the work of the Hall of Worthies was in the field of music, which Sejong loved and believed was vital to statecraft. It is due to him that much ancient ritual music is known today. He had the court's music master study the ceremonial music in an attempt to return to the classical inventions imported from China hundreds of years earlier, and it is these that can be heard at the annual rites conducted for the Chosŏn kings and for Confucius (*see* Rites for Royalty and Rites for Confucius in Beliefs and Customs). The traditional instruments imported from China were also improved and new ones created and a mensural notation for noting the duration of notes was also devised.

Always interested in scholarship, Sejong ordered the compiling of a great variety of scholarly works. *Straight Talk on Farming (Nongsa chiksŏl)*, a handbook on ways of storing seeds, improving seed fertility, planting and transplanting rice seedlings, and the like was compiled in 1430 after an extensive survey of each provincial district. *A Geographical Description of the Eight Provinces (P'alto chiri chi)*, the first attempt to make maps based on systematic surveys and measurements, was compiled in 1432 and included a wide variety of information about each local government district such as topographical features, land area, population, native products, roads, and more. In an effort to promote better government, Sejong had a manual for administrators made in 1441. Called *Exemplar of Efficient Government (Ch'ip'yŏng yoram)*, it provided guidance for officials with examples of administrative achievements and failures in the past.

Sejong also had made illustrated exemplary biographies drawn from Korean and Chinese history. They depicted the ideal behavior of loyal subjects, dutiful sons, virtuous wives, and appropriate relationships between superiors and inferiors. They were most influential in spreading the values that formed the basis of Confucian morality throughout all levels of Chosŏn society.

Compilations such as these led to great advancements in printing technology. One such improvement ordered by Sejong was the fashioning of type to fit into squares on metal printing plates. This improved the look of printed works because the type no longer shifted during printing as it had done when it was attached to the printing plates with beeswax and made possible the consecutive printing of many copies.

Medicine also saw great advancements during Sejong's reign. *Compilation of Native Korean Prescriptions (Hyangyak chipsŏng pang)*, with diagnostic methods and prescriptions for remedies, was made in 1433. It represented the liberation of Korean medical science from the Chinese; in other words, it established an independent Korean medical science based on Korean expertise. An encyclopedia of medicine followed in 1445.

In the field of agriculture, irrigation methods were improved with the introduction of various kinds of waterwheels and thousands of reservoirs and catch basins were constructed as drought relief measures. An improved armillary sphere and wind-direction and time indicators, including several types of improved water clocks, were introduced from 1432-38. Copper and iron rain gauges were made and distributed to the provincial districts in 1442, and accurate rainfall records began to be produced some 200 years before their compilation in the West.

Sejong also excelled in the area of national defense. With his well-trained army, he beat back Jurchen tribes and seized control of all lands south of the Yalu (Amnokkang) and Tumen (Tumangang) rivers. He had military posts and walled towns constructed in the new territories and moved settlers to them from the heavily populated southern provinces from 1431 to 1447. This essentially set the northern boundaries of what is now the modern Korean nation (the northern boundary of North Korea).

As for foreign relations, Sejong was not to be surpassed. His relationship with the suzerain state, Ming China, was perfect. The Ming emperors seemed charmed with him and every year sent him innumerable books and gifts. Great ministers went to

China as envoys and leading Chinese scholars made return visits. At the same time, Sejong increased trade with Japan by opening three ports to it.

Sejong ordered the compilation or revision of the official annals of the reigns of his three predecessors and established the procedures by which an official chronicle, or *shillok*, of each king's reign was to be compiled. He also began the practice of making extra copies for storing at branch archives in different regions of the country, and it is due to his foresight that the annals of the Chosŏn kings exist today, the main archives having been destroyed during the 1592-98 Japanese invasions.

Sejong was born in 1397. He was the third son of King T'aejong (r. 1400-18) who had twelve sons and seventeen daughters. Sejong became king at age twenty-one when his father abdicated in his favor. T'aejong chose Sejong to succeed him because his oldest son was inclined to drink and debauchery and his second son wished to become a Buddhist monk.

Shin Saimdang

The mother of the famous Neo-Confucian scholar Yi I (Yulgok, 1527-72; *see* entry in this chapter), Shin Saimdang (1504-51), nee Shin Yi-sŏn, is with all probability the most revered woman in all Korean history. She is considered the quintessential mother, wife, and daughter and an award named for her is presented to an outstanding woman each year.

She was born in the village of Pukpyŏng, which is now part of Kangnŭng City in Kangwon-do Province. Her father was an aristocrat named Shin Myŏng-hwa. She was the second of five daughters and had no brothers.

At a time when females were provided very little education, her parents educated her in the Confucian classics from an early age. She showed outstanding artistic talent from an early age and learned to paint by copying the works of master painters. At age nineteen, she married Yi Won-su, a distant relative of the famous naval hero Admiral Yi Sun-shin (*see* entry in this chapter). Contrary to custom and at the request of her father, she remained with her parents instead of going to live with her parents-in-law. Her father died the same year and she mourned for the customary three years. She then went to live with her husband's family in the village of Yulgok, which her famous son Yi I eventually took for his pen name. As her mother was living alone, she visited her as much as possible, which was very difficult as the two places were far apart over a difficult route. She helped her husband become a scholar. And, when he became a government official, he often discussed important matters with her and asked her advice because of her extensive knowledge of Confucian literature and the deeds of great sages.

They had four sons and three daughters. Their oldest daughter, Yi Maechang, achieved fame as a poet and a painter, and their fourth son, Yi U, excelled in poetry, calligraphy, painting, and playing *kŏmun-go* (Korean zither). Yulgok, their third and most famous child, was born when Saimdang was thirty-two. She personally saw to his education and by age seven he had mastered the Chinese classics, by eight he was writing poetry, and at age thirteen he passed a state civil service examination. Although Saimdang was a celebrated poet, calligrapher and painter, few examples of her work remain. She mostly depicted nature, painting fruits, flowers, grasses and insects in a style of her own.

Tan-gun

Koreans trace their history back thousands of years to the myths and mystery of shadowy prehistory to a man-god named Tan-gun. He was the son of Hwan-ung who was the son of Hwan-in, the God of All and ruler of Heaven. Hwan-ung longed to live among the mountains and valleys of Earth so his father sent him, accompanied by three thousand celestial helpers, to rule it and provide humans with much happiness.

Hwan-ung descended from Heaven to Mt. T'aebaeksan, or Mt. Paektusan as it is now known, on the border of Manchuria and

North Korea. He named the place Shinshi (City of God) and with his ministers of wind, rain and clouds, imposed a code of laws, and taught its inhabitants moral principles and more than three hundred useful arts including medicine and agriculture.

At the time there lived together in a cave a tiger and a bear who wished to become human. Hearing their prayers, Hwan-ung called to them and, giving them each twenty garlics and a bunch of mugwort, told them to eat the sacred food and stay out of the sunlight for a hundred days and their wish would be granted. The two then retired to the darkness of their cave. The tiger grew weary of the task and left the cave but the bear remained and after 21 days was transformed into a woman.

The bear-woman was thankful and made offerings to Hwan-ung. But soon she became sad because she had no companion. She could not find a husband so she prayed under a sandalwood tree to be blessed with a child. Moved by her prayers, Hwan-ung took her for his wife and they soon had a strong, handsome son and named him Tan-gun, meaning "Sandalwood" or "Altar Prince," depending on the Chinese characters and translation.

Tan-gun grew up to be wise and powerful. In 2333 B.C. he went to P'yŏngyang (the present capital of North Korea), established a residence and proclaimed his kingdom Chosŏn, Land of Morning Calm. He imparted to his people all the institutions of society and then, at the age of 1,908, he returned to Mt. Taebaek-san and became a mountain god.

Whether such a person actually existed is debatable but that Tan-gun is an important part of Korea's cultural heritage is not. Most Koreans, even those who believe him to be mythical, say that Tan-gun should be revered as a symbol of the Korean people and their culture. There are numerous religions that worship Tan-gun and more than thirty shrines to him throughout the country.

Wang Kŏn

Wang Kŏn (877-943) was the founder and first king of the Koryŏ Kingdom. He was from a wealthy seafaring merchant family of Songdo, which is today's Kaesŏng, North Korea. He was a pious Buddhist and a shrewd judge of human nature and politics.

He was born at a time when the Shilla Kingdom was far from united. The ruling class had grown to ignore the welfare of the people and the nation as a whole. The nobles ruled their own domains and had private armies and slaves. Under the clan system, their power had grown to such proportions that there were frequent clashes between them.

At the beginning of the tenth century, Shilla was plagued with civil disturbances arising from conflicts between powerful landowners, rich trade merchants, lower level aristocrats, powerful landowners, and men who had been educated in China under the merit system. Bands of rebels threatened the very foundations of the state.

In 897, Kungye, a prince who had been banished from the Shilla palace, killed the leader of the rebel army he had joined and assumed leadership. He then established his own monarchy and called it Latter Koguryŏ. He came to control most of the Shilla territory north of the Han River.

Wang Kŏn was in the army at the time. He became a favorite of Kungye's and was appointed governor of his hometown of Songdo. As governor, he grew strong and powerful as he was well liked by the people.

Kungye reigned with terror. He perpetuated untold abuses and instituted no reforms. He even killed his wife and children. As he became more and more tyrannical, the people turned to Wang Kŏn to save them from the monster. At first, Wang Kŏn refused on the grounds that he had sworn an oath of allegiance to Kungye, but after much persuasion he finally gave into the people's wishes and allowed them to crown him king. On hearing the news, Kungye fled to a cave but was hunted out by the country people and beaten to death. Wang Kŏn named his kingdom Koryŏ, meaning "high hills and sparkling waters."

At the same time, there was another rebel leader called General Kyŏnhwon. He rose up against Queen Chinsŏng (r. 887-897) whose decadence and immorality caused deep concern among many true patriots and scholars. In 892, Kyŏnhwon and his followers proclaimed the Latter Paekche Kingdom and established their capital at today's Chŏnju, Chŏllabuk-do Province.

For several decades, Kyŏnhwon and his armies harassed Koryŏ and Shilla. In 927, they sacked the Shilla capital and forced King Kyŏngae (r. 924-927) to fall on his own sword and put Kyŏngsun (r. 927-935) on the throne.

As Kyŏnhwon grew old, he began to have trouble with his own household. He designated his fourth and favorite son as heir to the throne. However, his eldest son seized the throne, killed the designated heir, and imprisoned Kyŏnhwon in a nearby Buddhist temple. Kyŏnhwon escaped and fled to Koryŏ. He asked Wang Kŏn for asylum in Songdo and protection against his own children. Wang Kŏn granted him asylum and even gave him a house and servants.

In the meantime, Shilla had officially recognized Koryŏ in 920 and even sent an envoy to Songdo. And, in 927, following Kyŏnhwon's sacking of the Shilla capital, Wang Kŏn sent condolences to Kyŏngsun and visited him the next year.

Kyŏngsun wanted to abdicate and turn Shilla over to Wang Kŏn as the kingdom had no strength to protect itself. However, opinions in the court were divided. Kyŏngsun finally abdicated in 935 and Shilla surrendered to Koryŏ.

Wang Kŏn appointed Kyŏngsun governor of Kyŏngju. He also took a woman from Shilla royalty as a wife and presented his own daughter to Kyŏngsun in marriage, symbolically legalizing his rule and his kingdom.

Wang Kŏn ruled for seven more years until he died in 943 at age sixty-five. Following the style of Chinese royalty, he was given the posthumous title T'aejo, meaning "Grand Progenitor," the name by which he is known to history. The dynasty he established in 918 ruled the Korean peninsula for 475 years.

Wonhyo

Wonhyo (617-684), one of the most eccentric figures in Korean history, was an itinerant Buddhist monk and scholar at the time Shilla unified the Korean Peninsula. Though he violated every standard for the normal monk, even fathering a child (Sŏl Ch'ong, a great scholar and literary figure) by Princess Yosŏk, he was revered as a saint. He popularized Buddhism among the masses by bringing the teachings of the Buddha out of the temples and monasteries to the people in the streets. His efforts supposedly brought about the conversion to Buddhism of more than 80 percent of the Shilla population.

At the time, there were many Buddhist sects but Wonhyo did not adhere to or condemn any of them. Instead he advocated viewing Buddhist doctrine from a higher level of abstraction to achieve a harmonious integration of the differing points of view among the various sects.

Realizing that the people were suffering from an acute sense of alienation resulting from Shilla's unification of Paekche and Koguryŏ, Wonhyo wrote a commentary to the Lotus Sutra that provided a starting point for national solidarity. With the analogy of the Buddha teaching three different disciples in three different ways, which were but transient means to be contained in one eternal truth, he explained the worth of unifying the three kingdoms, each of which was incomplete until it was contained in one entity.

Wonhyo's method of propagating Buddhism was eccentric and highly effective. He traveled around the country as a vagabond, carrying a *kŏmun-go* (6-string zither; *see* Music and Dance) which he played as he sang songs he composed to teach Buddhism. He preached to the common people about the hope of Pure Land Buddhism (Chŏngt'o pulgyo) and the cult of Amitabha, the saviour Buddha.

Wonhyo was born into a provincial family by the name of Sŏl in 617. He was ordained a monk at age twenty-nine. He increased his knowledge of Buddhism by visiting many revered masters and through self-study. He wrote over 240 books on

Buddhism, including commentaries and annotations to most of
the major sutra.

Yi Hwang, T'oegye

Often called the Chu Hsi of Korea, Yi Hwang (1501-70), or
T'oegye as he is better known by his pen name, was the foremost
Confucianist philosopher of his day. His explication and further
elaboration of the thought of the Chinese philosopher Chu Hsi
greatly influenced Korean thought and is still studied today.

Chu Hsi put Confucian teachings on a new metaphysical
foundation. He divided all existence into two interdependent
and inseparable components: *li*, or *i* in Korean (principle or reason), the formative element that accounts for what things are
and how they behave, or should behave normatively; and, *ch'i*,
or *ki* in Korean (vital force or matter), the energizing or concretiz-
ing element that gives things their individual form or character.

Based on Chu Hsi's dualistic theory, two schools of Neo-Confucian thought developed in Korea. One, the Churi-p'a, or Principle First School, emphasized the primacy of *i*, and the other,
the Chugi-p'a, or Matter First School, emphasized the primacy of
ki.

Yi Hwang was the greatest exponent of the *i* school. It was so
strongly affected by his philosophy that it is often referred to as
T'oegyehak, using his pen name. He stressed the role of *i* as the
basis of the activity of *ki* and defined the role of *i* in the function
of the human psyche. He emphasized the cultivation of moral
character, learning and reflection to perfect the self and ultimate-
ly achieve a moralistic society.

A dedicated educator, Yi Hwang established an academy
(sŏwon) at his birthplace near Andong after he left officialdom.
Drawn by his wisdom and scholarly achievements, students
came from every part of the country to be taught by him,
prompting King Sŏnjo (r. 1567-1608) to personally charter the
academy, giving it the name Tosan Sŏwon (Edification Mountain
Academy).

Through Yi Hwang's many books and disciples, who counted

well over three hundred, the study of Neo-Confucianism blossomed in Korea in the sixteenth century. His school of thought also exerted a great influence on Confucian scholarship in Japan and eventually constituted a main stream in Japanese Confucian thought.

Yi Hwang's thought has transcended the boundaries of the Orient and is now pursued in the West as well.

Yi I, Yulgok

The son of Shin Saimdang (*see* entry in this chapter), an esteemed woman artist and poet, Yi I, or Yulgok as he is better known by his pen name, was a famous philosopher and statesman in the sixteenth century. Against his will, he was called to office time and time again and at age forty-four he was made the vice director of the Royal Academy. He put forth many reform proposals in regard to government, the economy, and national defense. With prophetic vision, he urged the training of a hundred thousand troops to prepare for the future, but his words were ignored and shortly after his death Korea was invaded by the troops of Japanese warlord Toyotomi Hideyoshi. He wrote many books dealing with Confucian thought and also many poems.

Like his rival Yi Hwang (*see* entry in this chapter), Yi I based his thought on Chu Hsi's dualistic theory of *i* (reason; called *li* in Chinese) and *ki* (vital force or matter; *ch'i* in Chinese). However, while Yi Hwang emphasized the primacy of *i* as the fundamental factor in the existence of all the universe, Yi I emphasized the primacy of *ki*, claiming it was the controlling agent and prime mover of *i*. He said that *i* was generated by *ki* and so *ki* was responsible for the generation, maintenance, and purification of the values of the mind. He thus stressed the importance of practical affairs and the importance of searching for moral principles. He stressed looking outward rather than inward, and perceiving things from an intellectual perception rather than a spiritual perception.

Yi Sŏng-gye

Yi Sŏng-gye (1335-1408) founded the Chosŏn Kingdom and the Yi Dynasty that ruled it. Like his father, he was a military man. He rose to prominence at a time when the Koryŏ Kingdom was in the throes of social and political turmoil and was beset with attacks by Japanese raiders and diplomatic troubles with the newly established Ming China. He distinguished himself in repeated successes against Japanese raiders and came to enjoy great influence in the Koryŏ capital, especially among Neo-Confucianists.

In 1388, the Ming court proclaimed its intention of laying claim to Koryŏ's northeastern territory which the Mongols had occupied during their earlier domination of Korea. Troops were quickly mobilized and General Yi was ordered to lead an expedition against Ming China. At the mouth of the Yalu River, Yi, who opposed the expedition from the beginning, turned his army around and marched back to the Koryŏ capital. In a nearly bloodless coup, he and his troops ousted King U (r. 1374-88), and placed U's son (King Ch'ang; r. 1388-89) on the throne.

Yi immediately set about establishing a thorough reform. Within a year or so, Yi and his supporters, mainly the newly risen literati class, most of whom were advocates of Neo-Confucianism, deposed King Ch'ang and placed another member of the royal Wang house (King Kongyang; r. 1389-92) on the throne. Throughout the Koryŏ period, Confucianism and Buddhism had coexisted with little conflict, but the young scholars, imbued with the new Neo-Confucianism, did not agree with the Buddhist idea that one should denounce one's family ties to become a monk, strong family and social relationships being the very basis of Confucian philosophy. Moreover, the Buddhist establishment had amassed great estates and wealth and Buddhism was blamed for the decline of the kingdom as a result of corrupt monks meddling in affairs of state. Yi thus undertook a sweeping land reform.

First, a survey of landholding was made throughout the country and, in 1390, all registers of public and private land were destroyed and the Rank Land Law (Kwajŏnpŏp) was instituted. Under this law, land in the region around the capital was allocated to members of the official class in accordance with their rank. The rest of the land in the country was decreed state land; in a word, the estates of the powerful families and Buddhist temples were confiscated. The increase in state land resulted in increased government revenue, which gave Yi the economic means to found a new ruling house.

Of course, there were powerful opponents to Yi taking the throne. The most ardent was the highly revered Neo-Confucian scholar-official Chŏng Mong-ju (*see* entry in this chapter). Chŏng was a great friend and admirer of Yi and supported his land reform. However, he refused to accept the advent of a new dynasty because Confucian tradition made no allowance for a switch of loyalty to another sovereign by revolt. He was assassinated by Yi's fifth son, Yi Pang-won (1367-1422), who later ruled from 1400-18 and is known by the dynastic name T'aejong. In 1392, Kongyang (r. 1389- 92), the last king of the Koryŏ house of Wang, was forced to abdicate and Yi Song-gye took the throne.

Yi called his kingdom Chosŏn, Land of Morning Calm, after the most ancient Korean kingdom, and moved his capital to Hanyang, today's Seoul. He ruled until 1398 when he abdicated. He died in 1408 and was given the posthumous title T'aejo, meaning "Grand Progenitor," the name by which he is known to history. The dynasty he established ruled the Korean peninsula for 518 years.

Yi Sun-shin

Korea's most popular hero, Yi Sun-shin (1545-98) turned the tide of Asian history by decisively defeating the Japanese fleet during the Imjinwoeran, the 1592-98 Japanese invasions of Korea which were led by warlord Toyotomi Hideyoshi.

Hideyoshi's forces landed at Pusan on the southern coast in the spring of 1592. They overran the country, routed the ill-equipped Korean army and occupied the capital, causing the king, Sŏnjo (r. 1567-1608), to flee to China. Fortunately, Yi Sun-shin had been building warships and training crews to man them since his appointment as Naval Commander of Left Chŏlla the previous year. He modeled his ships, called *kŏbuksŏn*, meaning "turtle ship," after a model in use in the mid-fifteenth century.

The *kŏbuksŏn* had a protective covering, believed to have been iron plated, with numerous spikes embedded in it to prevent the enemy from boarding. Around the entire circumference were cannons to enable attack from any side.

Yi Sun-shin's fleet was victorious in successive battles off the southern coast. The victories gave the Korean forces complete control of the sea lanes, thereby preventing the Japanese from moving north by sea to link up with their 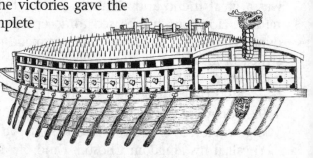 land armies and cutting off their supply routes.

However, Yi was later stripped of his title and rank as a target of factional conniving and the navy was put under the command of a rival, Won Kyun. The navy was virtually destroyed under Won's command. Yi was pardoned and again put in command of the navy, which had been reduced to twelve ships. Employing ingenious tactics, Yi led his small fleet against a Japanese fleet of 133 ships and won, marking a turning point in the war.

Hemmed in by land and sea, the Japanese began withdrawing from the peninsula. Attacking the retreating Japanese forces to the end, Yi was mortally wounded by a stray bullet in a battle in the narrow strait of Noryang. Before he died, Yi ordered that his death not be revealed until the fight was over lest it demoralize his men and result in defeat.

Yi Sun-shin was born in Seoul in 1545. He grew up in Asan, Ch'ungch'ŏngnam-do where his father, a Neo-Confucian scholar, moved to escape the political intrigues of the capital when Yi was eight years old.

Yu Kwan-sun

Yu Kwan-sun (1902-1920) was an independence fighter during the Japanese colonial period who is often called Korea's Joan of Arc. She was arrested for her anti-Japanese activities and, at age eighteen, she was beaten, tortured and stabbed to death in a Japanese prison in Seoul.

She was instrumental in spreading the news about the Samil Undong (March First Independence Movement; *see* entry in Miscellaneous) throughout the country in 1919. She built a signal fire high atop a mountain near her home in Yongdu-ri, Ch'ŏnwŏn-gun, Ch'ungch'ŏngnam-do Province to notify people in the surrounding areas about the March First activities. Her message was relayed via a series of mountaintop signal fires to other parts of the country. She also gathered more than three thousand people together in the marketplace of her hometown, distributed Korean flags, which were banned by the Japanese, and made a touching speech about the need for Korea to be independent and urging the people to take to the streets to demand independence.

At the time, she was attending Ewha Haktang, the predecessor of today's Ewha Womans University, which, like other missionary-run schools, encouraged patriotism and anti-Japanese resistance.

FAMOUS PLACES AND MONUMENTS

Buddhist Temples

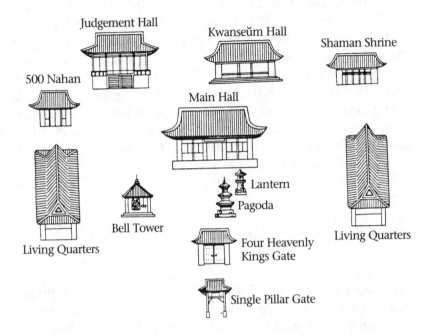

The temple, or *chŏl*, is the place where Buddhas *(Puch'ŏ)*, Boddhisattvas *(Posal)* and various saints and spirits are worshipped and venerated (*see* Buddhist Deities in Beliefs and Customs).

No two temples are alike though they all share similar features such as proliferating patterns of mineral colors called *tanch'ŏng* (*see* entry in Arts and Crafts), large images of Buddhas and Bodhisattvas, statues and paintings of fierce-looking guardians, icons, and various stone monuments including pagodas, stupas and lanterns. Large temples generally have a stone bridge, two or more gates, a main hall where Buddha is worshipped, a judgment hall housing statues of the Ten Kings of Hell where funerals are held, a hall containing from sixteen to five hundred images of arhats (*nahan:* disciples of Buddha), a hall to Avalokitesvara (Kwanseŭm posal), one or more Shamanist or Taoist inspired shrines, a bell pavilion and several pagodas and lanterns. Some temples also have living quarters, meditation and lecture halls, and hermitages.

The inner and outer walls of the halls are adorned with paintings. Among the most obvious are the *Palsangdo* and the *Shimudo*. The *Palsangdo, Eight Paintings from Sakyamuni's Life*, present Buddha's birth in the Lumbini Gardens; his childhood bath in the fire of nine dragons; his meditation in the mountains; his struggles with Mara (Mawang), the devil; his enlightenment under the Boddhi tree; scenes of him teaching; his death; and, his passage into Nirvana. The *Shimudo*, or *Ox Herding Paintings*, is a set of paintings illustrating the stages of spiritual progress toward Buddhahood or enlightenment. The number of paintings varies, but the series is easily identified by the ox which gradually turns white.

Ch'angdŏkkung Palace

The Palace of Illustrious Virtue, Ch'angdŏkkung was originally built in 1405 by T'aejong (r. 1400-18), the third ruler of Chosŏn, to be a royal villa, which is why it is not of the classic square layout. It was destroyed by fire during the 1592 Japanese invasions and rebuilt from 1607-10. Kwanghaegun (r. 1608-23) made it the seat of government in 1615 and it remained so until 1868 when Kojong (r. 1863-1907) began to reign from the newly rebuilt Kyŏngbokkung. It fell into disuse until 1907 when Sunjong, Korea's last monarch, made it the seat of government upon ascending the throne.

Ch'angdŏkkung is the best preserved of all the palaces. Tonhwamun, its main gate, is Seoul's oldest original gate. It was built in 1412 and escaped the various fires that ravaged the palace as well as the destruction of the Korean War. The throne hall, Injŏngjŏn, Hall of Benevolent Government, was first built in 1405, suffered several fires and was last rebuilt in 1804. A spectacular screen rich in symbolism stands behind its elaborate throne.

In the northeast part of the palace is a tranquil woodland which has been called Piwon, or Secret Garden, since the Japanese colonial period (1910-45). First landscaped as a rear garden in 1405 and subsequently enlarged in 1623, it is an excellent example of the most characteristic features of Korean garden aesthetics. Footpaths meander past ponds and streams to reach twenty-eight pavilions and other structures scattered about the garden's 78 acres.

Ch'anggyŏnggung Palace

The Palace of Glorious Blessings, Ch'anggyŏnggung stands on the site of a Koryŏ palace that T'aejo (r. 1392-98), the founder of Chosŏn, used until Kyŏngbokkung was constructed. Ch'anggyŏnggung was built by King Sejong (r. 1418-50) in 1418 as a residence for his father, King T'aejong (r. 1400-18), who had abdicated in his favor. It was called Suganggung until 1484 when, after many years of disuse, it was renovated and greatly enlarged to house the widowed queens of kings Sejo (r. 1455-68) and Yejong (r. 1468-69) and the name was changed to Ch'anggyŏnggung. Some of the buildings were destroyed during the 1592-98 Japanese invasions and later rebuilt in 1616. Much of the palace was destroyed in a fire in 1830 and reconstructed in 1834. A zoo and a botanical garden were opened to the public on the palace grounds in 1909. A 2-story building to house the Royal Yi Household Museum was built on the grounds in 1911 and the palace was renamed Ch'anggyŏng-won, demoting it from palace (*kung* or *gung*) to garden or park *(won)*. The palace underwent a major restoration from 1983-86 to remove the zoo and other amusement facilities and reconstruct many of the buildings which had been destroyed. It was renamed Ch'anggyŏnggung at that time.

The throne hall, Myŏngjŏngjŏn, Hall of Government by Intelligence, was constructed in 1483. It escaped the 1592 conflagrations and is therefore the oldest of all the throne halls in Seoul. It faces east like the throne halls of Koryŏ palaces instead of south like those of the Yi Dynasty.

Ch'ŏmsŏngdae Observatory

The bottle-shaped Ch'ŏmsŏngdae in Kyŏngju, the capital of the ancient Shilla Kingdom (57 B.C.-A.D. 935), is believed to be the oldest astronomical observatory in Asia. Korea's oldest secular structure, it is especially intriguing in that it is made of 362 stones, the number of days in a lunar calendar year, and there are 12 rows of stones above a window in its south side and 12 rows of stones below, which some scholars believe correspond to the number of months in a year and the number of animals in the Oriental zodiac.

Chongmyo Shrine

The royal ancestral shrine of the Yi Dynasty, Chongmyo houses the spirit tablets of the kings of Chosŏn and their queens and the tablets of those who were given the title of king or queen posthumously. It was first established in 1395, soon after Yi T'aejo, the founder king of Chosŏn, moved his capital from Songdo, today's Kaesŏng, North Korea, to Hansŏng, today's Seoul. He enshrined in it the spirit tablets of four generations of his ancestors which he brought from Kaesŏng.

The shrine comprises two buildings: Chŏngjŏn, which houses the spirit tablets of the kings who left direct heirs to the throne, and Yŏngnyŏngjŏn, which houses the tablets of those who died without direct heirs or who were honored posthumously with the title of king. There is a cubicle for each king and it contains his spirit tablet, the spirit tablets of his queen and other immediate family members, his personal seal, and his favorite books.

An unusually long building with wings at both sides and a

straight uninterrupted roof, Chŏngjŏn stands on an elevated platform of packed earth faced with stone and is fronted by a large cobbled plaza. It was first built in 1395, enlarged during the reign of Myŏngjong (r. 1545-67), destroyed during the sixteenth century Japanese invasions, and rebuilt in 1608. It was enlarged by Yŏngjo (r. 1724-76), again by Hŏnjong (r. 1834-49), and finally to its present size by Kojong (r. 1863-1907). Forty-nine tablets including those of T'aejo (r. 1392-98), the founder of Chosŏn and its Yi Dynasty, Sejong (r. 1418-50), who is credited with the invention of the Korean alphabet, and Kojong (r. 1863-1907) and Sunjong (r. 1907-10), the last rulers of Chosŏn, are enshrined in Chŏngjŏn.

Thirty-three tablets including those of T'aejo's father, grandfather, great-grandfather, and great-great-grandfather and the last crown prince Yŏngch'in-wang, who died on May 1, 1970, are enshrined in Yŏngnyŏngjŏn. The building is similar to Chŏngjŏn, but the center, which houses the tablets of T'aejo's ancestors, is raised higher than the wings. It was constructed by King Sejong in 1421, burnt down during the sixteenth century Japanese invasions, reconstructed in 1608, and later expanded.

Near the front of the courtyard of Chŏngjŏn is a structure called Kongshindang where the tablets of eighty-three ministers of state and others recognized for meritorious service are enshrined. Other structures include a building originally built for musicians to rehearse, rest or wait for a performance and one built to prepare the food and utensils necessary for the memorial rites.

Throughout the Chosŏn period (1392-1910), Confucian rites called *chehyang* (*see* Rites for Royalty in Beliefs and Customs) were held five times a year for those enshrined in Chŏngjŏn and twice a year for those enshrined in Yŏngnyŏngjŏn. The rites were abolished in the early part of the twentieth century but were resumed in 1969, though in the form of one large service. The annual service is held on the first Sunday in May by the Chŏnju Yi Clan Association, the clan to which the royal Yi family belonged.

Confucian Shrines

There are many ancient Confucian shrines scattered throughout the Korean countryside. They were constructed as a place to venerate Confucius and his disciples and many of them also functioned as academies.

The shrine-academies can be divided into two types: *hyanggyo* and *sŏwon*. *Hyanggyo* were public schools established in major provincial towns and cities by the government to promote Confucian education. *Sŏwon* were private schools established in provincial areas by Confucian scholars. *Sŏwon,* which preserved and developed a particular line of Confucian thinking and created a body of men dedicated to its political implementation, served to develop the political power of the Confucian literati. A *sŏwon* usually contained a shrine to its founding scholar.

The buildings and layout of Korean Confucian shrines generally follow the architectural principles of Chinese prototypes. The shrine compound is surrounded by a wall and entered through a triple gate in the south face of the wall. The buildings are oriented along a north-south axis. The main gate opens to a square of buildings with a courtyard in the middle. Facing the gate is the shrine building and running longitudinally on the east and west are subsidiary buildings. All of the buildings are raised off the ground on terraces of pounded earth.

Hyanggyo and *sŏwon* have a second walled compound in front of the shrine building, or beside it. Facing the gate across a courtyard is a lecture hall and running longitudinally on the east and west are subsidiary buildings such as dormitories and libraries.

Kyŏngbokkung Palace

The Palace of Shining Happiness, Kyŏngbokkung was constructed in 1395 when Yi T'aejo, the founder-king of the Chosŏn Kingdom, decided to move the capital to Hansŏng, today's Seoul, from Songdo, now Kaesŏng, North Korea, the capital of the previous Koryŏ Kingdom. It was the home of kings and the principal site of royal audiences and other court functions until 1592 when it was destroyed by fire during the 1592-98 Japanese invasions led by Toyotomi Hideyoshi. Because the site was considered inauspicious, the palace was left in ruins until 1865, when the Prince Regent Taewon-gun, the father of King Kojong (r. 1863-1907), ordered it reconstructed to its original grandeur. The reconstruction was completed in 1868.

Most of the palace's two hundred buildings were torn down after Japan annexed Korea in 1910. A large granite building to house the Japanese government-general was built on the palace grounds directly in front of the main throne hall, Kŭnjŏngjŏn. The building was the headquarters of the American Military Government from 1945 until the establishment of the Republic of Korea in 1948, at which time the building became the Republic's capitol. In 1950 it was set afire by North Koreans retreating after General Douglas MacArthur's landing at Inch'ŏn. It remained a gutted hulk until the early 1960s when it was refurbished to house the offices of the central government. The capitol was eventually relocated in 1983 and, after the building was renovated and enlarged, it became the home of the National Museum of Korea in 1986.

Kŭnjŏngjŏn, the main throne hall, faces south down the main axis of the city. It is said that in the old days Namdaemun (South Gate), which is about one and a quarter miles away, was visible from the throne. Stone fire-eating beasts called *haet'ae* stand at the steps and the corners of the stone railings to protect the double-roofed hall from fire. To each side of the royal walkway leading to the throne is a row of inscribed stone tablets marking the position of the court and military officials, the highest rank being closest to the hall.

Munmyo, Temple of Confucius

Munmyo is a shrine honoring Confucius and a number of other Chinese and Korean champions of Confucianism. It and the national Confucian academy Sŏnggyun-gwan (*see* Sŏnggyun-gwan in this chapter) were the focal point of Confucian ceremony and study during the Chosŏn period (1392-1910). It is located on the campus of Sung Kyun Kwan University, * the descendant of Sŏnggyun-gwan.

The Munmyo compound follows the principles of Chinese prototypes. It is surrounded by a wall with the main entrance, a triple gate, in its south face. The buildings are oriented along a north-south axis with subsidiary buildings running longitudinally on the east and west.

The main shrine Taesŏngjŏn (Hall of Great Accomplishments), or Munmyo as it is sometimes called, is the most important building in the compound but the Myŏngnyundang (Hall of Illuminating Ethics) lecture hall is the largest. They were first constructed in 1398, burnt down in 1400 and rebuilt in 1407. They were again destroyed during the 1592-98 Japanese invasions. The Taesŏngjŏn was rebuilt in 1601 and the Myŏngnyundang in 1606 with funds raised by students of Sŏnggyun-gwan. General repairs were made to the buildings in 1869.

Rites honoring Confucius and his disciples have been held at the Munmyo in the spring and autumn since 1398. During the Chosŏn period (1392-1910), 131 Chinese and Koreans were honored along with Confucius. Now only Confucius, his four closest associates, ten philosophers he highly praised, six Sung Chinese sages who developed the Neo-Confucian doctrine which became the only orthodox doctrine in Korea, and eighteen Korean sages are honored with the rites which are called *sŏkchŏn* (*see* Rites for Confucius in Beliefs and Customs).

Namdaemun Gate

National Treasure No. 1, Namdaemun (Great South Gate) was the main entrance to the capital city during the Chosŏn period

---

* This is the way the university spells its name.

(1392-1910). It was first built
in 1398 when the city
wall was constructed
but it had to be torn
down and rebuilt in
1448 because it did
not settle properly.
It was burnt dur-
ing the Korean
War (1950-53),

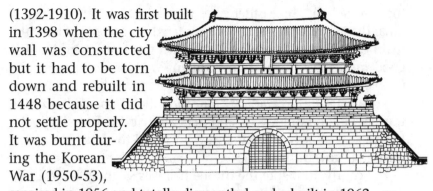

repaired in 1956 and totally dismantled and rebuilt in 1962.

Namdaemun is the best preserved and most famous of the five gates that remain of the nine gates that once led through the wall that encircled the city. Its formal name is Sungnyemun, Gate of Exalted Ceremonies, which can be seen in Chinese characters on a plaque underneath its uppermost eaves.

The base of the gate is made of granite blocks and has one arched passageway. The top of the gate is a wooden, 2-story pavilion with a hipped roof.

Palaces

Korean palaces *(kunggwol)* were laid out according to Chinese concepts reflecting the ruler's position between Heaven and Earth; he was thought to be the Son of Heaven, ruling by a mandate from Heaven and responsible for all the Earth. Koreans viewed their own king as the younger brother of the Chinese emperor and having a similar relation to Heaven and Earth. The primary purpose of the king's palace was thus to be an auspicious center from which he could transmit the will of Heaven to his subjects.

Palaces faced south, the direction believed to be the source of *yang,* or positive force. They were made up of several sections. The grand entrance to the throne hall, the throne hall and its front courtyard and the residential quarters were the most important. The main gate opened onto the courtyard in front of the throne hall. Three other gates were located at one of the cardinal directions. The palace was centered on an axis around the main gate and the throne hall because it was from them that the good influences of royal government were to flow out to the people. The name of the main palace gate thus always contained the character *hwa,* meaning "transformation," to symbolize the transfer of good influences, and the name of the throne hall, the formal seat of government, always included the character *chŏng,* meaning "government."

The courtyard before the throne hall was surrounded by corridors on three sides. The corridors extended from both sides of the main gate. A walkway with a raised center extended from the gate to the throne hall. The center of the walkway was reserved for the king. On each side of the walkway were rows of stones marking the positions for high civil and military officials to stand for royal audiences.

The informal aspects of government were conducted in buildings behind or to the side of the throne hall. Structures related to the daily life of the royal family were behind the halls of government. These included residences for the king and for the queen and places for recreation and pleasure.

In addition to the formal state palace, there were detached palaces where the royal family could relax away from state affairs and where other members of the royal family might live. There was usually a palace to the east of the formal palace for the crown prince. All of the detached palaces had throne halls.

See:
Ch'angdŏkkung
Ch'anggyŏnggung
Kyŏngbokkung
Tŏksugung

Pagoda Park

This small park in the heart of Seoul was laid out as the first public park in Korea by Sir John MacLeavy Brown of the Customs

Service around the turn of the nineteenth century. It is famous because the Samil Undong independence movement against Japanese colonial rule (*see* March First Independence Movement in Miscellaneous) began here with the reading of the Korean Declaration of Independence on March 1, 1919.

The park is named for a beautiful 10-story pagoda which is one of only a couple of remains of Won-gaksa, a Buddhist temple founded on the site in 1464. However, Won-gaksa was predated by a temple called Hŭngdŏksa which was razed some time after the reign of King T'aejo (r. 1392-98) when other temples in the capital were destroyed because of a Confucian bias against Buddhism.

Won-gaksa was built by King Sejo (r. 1455-68) out of remorse for usurping the throne from his nephew, King Tanjong (r. 1452-55), and having him murdered. It was apparently enormous as the roof of its main hall was supported by three hundred columns. Yŏnsan-gun (r. 1494-1506) turned the temple into a school for training *kisaeng* (*see* entry in Miscellaneous) and for his own ribaldry. Chungjong (r. 1506-44) moved the temple bell to Namdaemun Gate (*see* entry in this chapter) and razed the buildings. The place remained in ruins until it was made into the park.

Pulguksa

One of the largest, oldest and most famous temples in Korea is Pulguksa, whose name means "Temple of the Buddha Land." However, its fame comes not from its size or age but from its beauty as an outstanding example of ancient Korean architecture.

Built on a series of stone terraces, the temple appears to emerge organically from the rocky terrain of the wooded foothills of Mt. T'ohamsan near the historic city of Kyŏngju. It is at once monolithic and intricate and takes on different guises with shifts in light, shadow, and weather.

The temple dates to a small temple King Pŏphŭng (r. 514-540), the first Shilla ruler to adopt Buddhism as a state religion, had erected for his queen to pray for the prosperity and peace of the kingdom. However, the present structures date to 757 when Kim Tae-sŏng, the chief minister at the time, built Pulguksa on the spot. The stonework, including the foundations, staircases, platforms, and several pagodas, dates from that time, but the wooden edifices date from 1973 when the temple was completely restored.

The temple has many masterpieces of Shilla architecture, sculpture and craftsmanship including six National Treasures and one Treasure.

Sajiktan

The Sajiktan is two altars where kings of the Chosŏn Kingdom made ritual offerings to the gods of Earth and Harvest on behalf of the nation. Their location was one of the first sites determined when King T'aejo (*see* Yi Sŏng-gye in Historic Figures) laid out his new capital, today's Seoul, in 1394.

The offerings, which included slaughtered animals, were performed in spring and autumn (in the second and eighth lunar months). Special offerings were sometimes made, for example, in time of drought. As with other forms of rites, the offerings were made according to prescribed rituals.

The name of the altars was changed to T'aejiktan (Great Altars to Earth and Harvest) in 1897 when King Kojong (r. 1863-1907) proclaimed the Taehan Empire and changed his title to emperor. From that time, offerings were also made at the winter solstice.

The Sajiktan is located in the Sajik Park which is located a few blocks west of Kyŏngbokkung Palace (*see* entry in this chapter).

Sŏkkuram

A manmade grotto shrine designed around the worship of a principal statue of Buddha, Sŏkkuram sits high above Pulguksa Temple (*see* entry in this chapter) on the eastern slope of Mt. T'ohamsan near the historic city of Kyŏngju. A reflection of the application of advanced scientific principles and precise mathematical and architectural concepts, not to mention great technical skills, it is a religious work of art unsurpassed by any other in Korea.

Supposedly built in 751, at the same time as Pulguksa, it comprises a square antechamber and a round interior chamber with a domed ceiling connected by a rectangular passageway. In addition to the principle statue of a large seated Buddha in the rotunda, there are thirty-seven figures, mostly in high relief, arranged according to their function and rank in the Buddhist pantheon. Many of them are protectors of the main chamber in which the principal statue of Buddha is located. The Buddha is positioned in such a way that the first rays of the rising sun strike a jewel in its forehead. The Buddha is considered by many art historians to be the most perfect Buddhist statue in the world.

Sŏnggyun-gwan Academy

The predecessor of today's Sung Kyun Kwan University, the Sŏnggyun-gwan,* or Hall of Perfection and Equalization, was the national academy during the Chosŏn period (1392-1910). It administered the government examinations known as *kwagŏ* (*see* entry in Miscellaneous) which opened the way for official advancement throughout the period. It was constructed in 1398

---

* This is spelled according to McCune-Reischauer, the romanization system used throughout the book, while the university uses its own system of romanizing.

by order of T'aejo, the founder of the Chosŏn Kingdom and its Yi Dynasty, for the study of Confucian philosophy and the veneration of Confucius. It was named for a Chinese educational institution which existed in the Chinese capital during the Chou period (1111-221 B.C.).

However, a similar academy had been constructed around 1394 in Kaesŏng, the capital of Koryŏ, the kingdom Chosŏn replaced. It had been built on the advice of An Hyang (1243-1306), a leading scholar-official, and others of high political and academic standing who were convinced that the country would be improved by the promotion of Confucianism. At the time Koryŏ was ravaged by wars, the number of Buddhist temples far exceeded the spiritual needs of the people, and corrupt Buddhist monks interfered in state affairs. An Hyang sent an envoy to China to bring back materials to use in establishing the academy. They included portraits of Confucius and his disciples as well as musical instruments and other items for performing rites to them.

Although at one time those who passed the *kwagŏ* were accepted as residents and lived in dormitories which could accommodate two hundred, the Sŏnggyun-gwan was not a school in the sense that students took courses and graduated. It was an academy of learning where scholars gathered to discuss or debate the classics.

The institution functioned as the premier academy for Confucian studies until the *kwagŏ* system was abolished in 1895. It was reopened as an academy of classical studies by several Confucian scholars in the early twentieth century. It was made into a junior college during the Japanese colonial period of 1910-45 and it became a university in 1945.

Tŏksugung Palace

The Palace of Virtuous Longevity, Tŏksugung is said to have been first built by King Sŏngjong (r. 1469-94) as a villa for his elder brother, Prince Wolsan, somewhat as a consolation prize for having been passed over for the throne. It did not achieve prominence until 1593 when King Sŏnjo (r. 1567-1608), on returning to the capital from which he had fled during the 1592 Japanese invasions, used it as his palace because the other royal residences had been destroyed. It was called Sŏgung, or West Palace. Kwanghaegun (r. 1608-23), the next ruler, renamed the palace Kyŏng-un-gung, Palace of Good Fortune, and ruled from it until he moved to the rebuilt Ch'angdŏkkung Palace in 1615. He renamed it Sŏgung in 1618. Kwanghaegun was deposed by King Injo (r. 1623-49) in 1623. Injo's coronation was held here but he ruled from Ch'angdŏkkung. The palace remained a subsidiary palace until 1897, the year Kojong (r. 1863-1907) proclaimed himself emperor and moved here. Kojong expanded it to use as his primary palace and again called it Kyŏng-un-gung. Most of the palace was destroyed in an 11-day fire in 1904 and the king took up residence in the Chungmyŏngjŏn Library where, less than a year later, he was forced to sign a protectorate treaty with Japan that led to occupation. Kojong returned to the palace when its reconstruction was completed in 1906 but the following year he was forced by the Japanese to abdicate in favor of his son Sunjong (r. 1907-10). Sunjong moved the seat of government to Ch'angdŏkkung and Kojong continued to live at the palace which was renamed Tŏksugung, Palace of Virtuous Long Life, to honor him. Kojong died in the palace on January 22, 1919, touching off a nationwide independence movement.

Although the throne hall, Chunghwajŏn, Hall of Central Harmony, faces south, the palace is not of a classic layout and most of the buildings are not representative of traditional Chosŏn architectural styles. Some ancient scientific inventions, including one of the world's oldest water clocks, can be seen on the grounds.

Tombs, *Myo* and *Nŭng*

The basic form of any Korean tomb *(myo)*, regardless of historic period or the status of the occupant, is a mound. The corpse is placed in a trench in the ground, packed with clay, and covered with earth and sodded to form a mound. The site would have been selected in light of certain geomantic considerations (*see* Geomancy in Beliefs and Customs).

A tomb is usually surrounded by an earthen ridge on three sides, the east, west and north, to protect it from evil forces from those directions. Depending on family circumstances and the status of the occupant, there may be a stele or other stone monument *(pisŏk)* inscribed with the clan and name of the occupant and other relevant information, such as important achievements. Also, there is usually an altar in front of the tomb, and

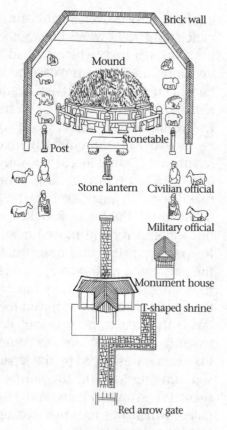

A Royal Tomb

there may be a small low stone table in front of it for burning incense and a small stone chair for the ancestral tablet. There may also be a stone lantern and in front and to the side of the tomb there may be some stone guardian figures in the form of civilian and military officials.

A royal tomb *(nŭng)* usually has a rather large mound compared to a commoner's tomb and is normally surrounded on the east, west and north by a stone wall. It always has the previously mentioned stele, altar, incense table, ancestral tablet chair, lantern and guardian figures as well as a red arrow gate *(hongsalmun)*, a stele pavilion *(pigak)*, a storehouse for ritual implements *(subokch'ŏng)*, a building for conducting the ritual sacrifices *(chŏngjagak)*, and a great number of stone figures of animals around its perimeter and in front of it. The red arrow gate, which marks off the sacred enclosure, stands in front of the tomb.

Tongdaemun Gate

Tongdaemun, Great East Gate, was the main entranceway on the east *(tong)* side of the capital city during the Chosŏn period (1392-1910). It was first built in 1398 when the city wall was constructed. It was rebuilt in its present form in 1869 and has since been repaired several times.

Tongdaemun is distinguished by a semicircular fortifying wall extending beyond the entranceway that enabled defenders to attack invaders on several sides. The fortifying wall, called *ongsŏng*, was a feature of gates of the Koryŏ period (1392-1910). The base of the gate is made of granite and has one arched entranceway. The top of the gate is a wooden 2-story pavilion with a hipped roof.

The formal name of the gate is Hŭng-injimun, Gate of Uplifting Mercy.

Tongnimmun

One of Korea's first Western-style structures, Tongnimmun, or Independence Arch as it is generally called in English, was erected in 1896 as a symbol of Korea's freedom from foreign domination. It was built by the Tongnip Hyŏphoe, a club dedicated to the cause of Korean independence. It is located in the Sŏdaemun district of Seoul at the site of Yŏng-ŭnmun, a gate where annual emissaries from China were greeted from

1539 until almost the end of the Chosŏn period (1392-1910). Two stone pillars in front of the arch are all that remain of Yŏng-ŭnmun.

Won-gudan

Until 1897, when King Kojong declared Korea an empire, no offerings were made to Heaven. This was because the system of royal Confucian rites reflected Korea's place in the cultural milieu of Chinese civilization. Korean kings viewed the emperor of China as the son of Heaven and thus in a position to make direct offerings to Heaven and viewed themselves as only younger brothers of the emperor and thus not worthy of making such offerings.

With the proclaiming of the Taehan Empire, an altar for making offerings to Heaven was erected and given the name Won-gudan. It was composed of three levels connected by steps and the top was sod. There was also a pavilion where ceremonial preparations were made.

The altar no longer exists but the pavilion, called Hwanggun-gu, Temple of the Imperial Firmament, remains at the rear of the Westin Chosun Hotel in downtown Seoul.

GAMES AND SPORTS

Ch'ajŏnnori, Juggernaut Battle

A mock battle between two teams wielding giant A-frames, *ch'ajŏnnori,* or *tongch'aessaum* as it is sometimes called, is a large-scale contest usually played at New Year's. It requires much preparation to make the large A-frames.

Each team sends several men out to select a tree to use to make the A-frame. Of course the tree must be purchased from the owner. Once the deal is struck, the men set out to cut it down and bring it home but only after preparing themselves by bathing, donning new clothes and paying homage to the Mountain Spirit (Sanshin).

After the A-frame is constructed a small platform is attached near the middle of the frame. A rope, or reins, is tied to the top of the A-frame for the captain to hold to as he stands on the platform.

Part of the team carries the A-frame while the rest of the team, arms crossed in front of them, push with their shoulders in a scrummaging fashion. Riding the A-frames, the team captains shout directions or signal with a flag. The object of the game is to make the tip of the opponent's A-frame touch the ground.

According to legend, this game was first played in celebration of a victorious battle Shilla forces fought against an army that tried to revive the Paekche Kingdom which it had defeated.

Changgi

One of the most popular board games in Korea, *changgi* is a variation of an ancient prototype of chess that was developed in China after being introduced from Mesopotamia where it is believed to have originated 4,500 years ago. It was introduced from China during the Koryŏ period (918-1392).

Changgi is a war between two camps of men led by a king or general, the object being to capture the opponent's king. It is played by two players on a square board that is marked off with

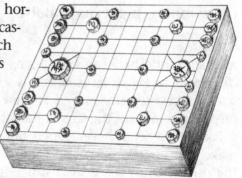

nine vertical lines and ten horizontal lines and has two castles, or *kung,* one for each side's king. Each player has sixteen pieces, or men, of seven different types, each type moving in a different way on the board. Each player has one king, two chariots, two cannons, two horses, two elephants, two knights and five soldiers.

The playing pieces are flat like checker pieces but octagonal, not round, and are inscribed with Chinese ideographs identifying each one. One set of pieces, called the Han Kingdom, has red lettering in a neatly printed style and the other, called the Cho Kingdom, has blue lettering in a hurried or cursive style called grass writing. The weaker player plays with the blue pieces and moves first. Sometimes a player who is much better than his opponent plays without one or two major pieces.

Chegi

Chegi refers to a shuttlecock Korean children, mostly boys, use in a kicking game that is called by the same name. There are many variations of the game but the object is the same: to keep the shuttlecock in the air.

The *chegi* is usually kicked using the instep of the foot. It can be kicked in one of three ways: with either foot and touching the ground between kicks; with either foot but not touching the ground between kicks; or kicking with alternate feet.

Chuldarigi, Tug of War

A village contest usually staged during the New Year season, *chul-darigi*, or tug of war, requires much preparation. Long before New Year's, villagers, divided into two teams, start to make small sections of rope which later will be joined to form a large rope.

On the day of the contest, the two teams, one called female and the other, male, carry their sections of rope to the contest site. The rope of the female team has a looped end and that of the male team, a fist-shaped end. These ends are fitted together to form a long rope and a flag is placed at the center. When all is ready, a gong signals the beginning of the contest. The first team to pull the rope toward its side wins.

The village is said to prosper in the coming year if the female team wins.

Hwat'u

One of the most popular forms of amusement in Korea is playing cards called *hwat'u*. The deck of forty-eight plastic match-book-size cards that is currently used is of Japanese origin and has been popular since the 1910-45 Japanese occupation of Korea. Koreans originally played with a deck of eighty long, narrow oil-paper cards bearing stylized Chinese characters indicating eight suits of animals.

There are twelve suits of four cards in a *hwat'u* deck. Each suit is named for a different month of the year and each card bears a flower or other natural phenomenon associated with that particular month. The suits and their motifs are: First Month, pine; Second Month, plum;

Third Month, cherry; Fourth Month, wisteria; Fifth Month, iris; Sixth Month, peony; Seventh Month, bush clover; Eighth Month, earth and sky; Ninth Month, chrysanthemum; Tenth Month, maple; Eleventh Month, paulownia; and Twelfth Month, rain. Five cards carry the Chinese ideogram for light and have a twenty-point value. Nine cards have a colorful symbol such as a bird as part of the month motif and have a ten-point value. Ten cards have a red or blue banner across them and have a five-point value.

Many games of varying complexity can be played with *hwat'u* cards. The cards are also used for fortunetelling.

Kiteflying, *Yŏnnalligi*

Kiteflying, or *yŏnnalligi* as it is called in Korean, has long been popular for Koreans, especially during the New Year's season. Kiteflying usually reaches its peak on the first full moon of the lunar year, which is called Taeborŭm (*see* entry in Special Days).

In the past, it was customary on Taeborŭm to write one's name, birthday and the phrase "Bad luck begone, good luck stay," on a kite, or *yŏn,* and let it fly away in the hope of ensuring good luck throughout the year. Those who flew kites after Taeborŭm were considered ill-bred.

The earliest record of kiteflying in Korea is in Korea's oldest history book, *Samguk sagi* (*see* entry in Language and Letters) published in 1145. According to it, a star fell from the sky in 637, the first year of the reign of Queen Chindŏk (r. 647-654) of the Shilla Kingdom against whom a rebellion was raging. The falling star was considered an ill omen against the Queen. So Kim Yu-shin (*see* entry in Historic Figures), the general trying to put down the revolt, sent a large burning kite into the sky at night and then circulated the story that the star had returned to heaven. Thus he succeeded in suppressing the rebellion.

Konggi

This girl's game, similar to Western jacks, is traditionally played with small round stones, *konggi,* but these days plastic and rubber *konggi* are mass produced. There are numerous versions of the game.

The most common version is played with five *konggi*. The player throws a *konggi* straight up in the air, picks up one of the *konggi* on the ground and catches the tossed one. The number of *konggi* to be picked up increases with each play. In the fifth play, the player must place all five *konggi* on the back of her hand, throw them into the air and catch them in her palm. Points are determined by the number of *konggi* caught.

Kossaum, Loop Fight

Played with two large loop-like rope structures, *kossaum* is a fast-paced pushing game. The object of the game is to push the other team's rope head to the ground.

The giant loop, which may be as long as 10 meters, is made of straw and wood. The rope to which it is attached is made of straw reinforced with sticks. The entire rope may be 100 meters long. Each team, usually fifty to eighty people, consists of a commander who rides on the loop, guards, five of whom protect the commander, pushers and a woman who controls the end of the rope.

The teams are designated male and female. The outcome of the game is believed to foretell the future of the village in the coming year. If the female team wins, the year will be productive.

Nŏlttwigi

A jumping game similar to see-sawing, *nŏlttwigi* is a traditional game played by girls and young women. It is especially popular at New Year's, when it affords the players a chance to show off their new clothes.

The see-saw is made by placing a rolled-up straw mat under a long board *(nŏl)*. Two girls play at a time by jumping at either end of the board. As one girl returns to the board, the other is propelled into the air.

Nŏlttwigi is said to have been very popular in the olden days because of the opportunity it provided women, who were not allowed outside the premises of their homes, to see over the walls of their houses.

Nottari palki, Princess Bridge

A women's game generally played on Taeborŭm (*see* entry in Special Days), the fifteenth day of the first lunar month, *nottari palki* came into being in the fourteenth century when King Kongmin (r. 1351-74) of the Koryŏ Kingdom took refuge in the Andong area during a civil rebellion. At the time, King Kongmin and his queen and princess had to cross a stream where there was no bridge. Women of all ages formed a human bridge by standing in a line and bending over so that the royal family could walk across their backs.

In Andong, where the game is very popular, women of all ages participate. The oldest women lead the others in a procession. Then the young women form a bridge of bended backs and a "princess," assisted by attendants, walks across the bridge while the older women sing. After the princess walks across, she joins the line and another princess walks across and joins the line, and another and another so that the bridge not only perpetuates but also moves.

Paduk

Known in the West by its Japanese name, *go, paduk* is perhaps the most popular board game played in Korea. It has been played in Korea for two thousand years and its mastery has long been considered the mark of a superior person. It is played professionally, with players competing for huge purses.

Paduk is a contest of wits between two players, one using black button-like markers and the other, white. The object of the game is to occupy more territory on the board than one's opponent. There is no front line, as in chess; the markers may be put down all over the board at the 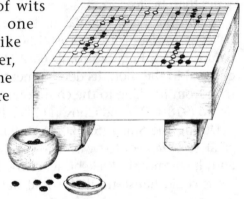 intersections of the nineteen vertical and horizontal lines which divide the board into small blocks. Play alternates between black and white with each player placing one stone at a time on any vacant intersection on the board. A stone is not moved again unless removed as a captive.

The action is governed by simple rules but involves highly complex strategies.

Ssirŭm, Wrestling

An unarmed, one-on-one combat sport, *ssirŭm* involves a variety of skills including grappling, tripping and throwing. Each wrestler binds his loins and the upper thigh of his right leg with a 2-foot-long cloth called *satpa;* one uses a red *satpa* and the other, blue. The wrestlers kneel down on the ground facing each other. Each wrestler grasps the other's *satpa* in the right hand at the loins and in the left hand at the thigh. At the referee's signal, the two wrestlers stand, pushing and pulling and employing a variety of tactics to try to throw the other to the ground. The first wrestler to touch the ground with any part of his body, other than his feet, loses.

Ssirŭm has been popular in Korea since ancient times. It is believed to date back at least 1,500 years, judging from a wall painting in a Koguryŏ tomb (c. A.D. 400) which depicts men engaged in the sport. Its development into a sport enjoyed by all men from the king to the commoner can be traced through the Koryŏ (918-1392) and Chosŏn (1392-1910) periods.

During the Shilla (57 B.C.-A.D. 935) and Koryŏ periods, the greatest *ssirŭm* contest was held on the fifteenth day of the seventh lunar month, Paekchung, or the Day of Servants, when servants could transcend their social status by proving their physical prowess. During the Chosŏn period, it became a major event of the festive programs of Tano (*see* entry in Special Days), the fifth day of the fifth lunar month, with the winner awarded the title "Super Strong Man" and an ox.

Ssirŭm continues to enjoy great popularity and is even included in middle and high school athletic programs. It is also played as a professional sport with matches held throughout the year and especially on national holidays and on Tano. However, competitions are now held in divisions based on weight.

Yut

A game derived from ancient divination rituals, *yut* is enjoyed by people of all ages and is traditionally played during the New Year season. It may be played by two people or by teams pitted against each other and requires four wooden sticks about 8 inches long with one flat side and one convex, a game board which may be drawn on paper or on the ground, and markers.

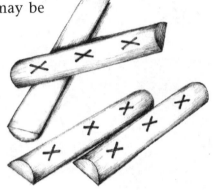

The object of the game is to move one's four men, or markers, completely around a circular or square diagram of twenty dots before the opponent is able to do the same. An interior cross of nine dots that intersects the diagram provides short cuts toward the end dot from which men can exit the diagram.

A player's move is determined by a toss of the *yut* sticks. The moves are: *mo,* a five-dot move, all four sticks fall convex side up; *yut,* a four-dot move, all four sticks fall round side up; *kŏl,* a three-dot move, three of the four sticks fall flat side up; *kae,* a two-dot move, two of the sticks fall flat side up; and *to,* one of the sticks falls flat side up. A toss of *mo* or *yut* entitles the player to another toss and the two tosses may be divided between two men.

If a player's man lands on a dot occupied by an opponent's man, the player takes another turn and the opponent's man must go back to the beginning and start over. If a player's man lands on a dot occupied by one of his own men, both men can move together on a single toss of the sticks.

MISCELLANEOUS

Hwarang, Flower of Youth Troop

The *hwarang* was a troop of young warriors, usually in their mid teens, organized to supplement the elite units that formed the core of Shilla's military forces. The *hwarang* were trained in martial arts and schooled in nationalism. They played a decisive role in Shilla's military successes.

The *hwarang*, or Flower of Youth Corps as it is often translated, originated in the sixth century or earlier but it was after its reorganization in the early six hundreds that it had its greatest impact. At that time, the monk Won-gwang, Shilla's highly esteemed spiritual leader who was well versed in both Buddhism and Confucianism, put forth five principles by which a Buddhist layman could live: to be loyal to the sovereign, to be filial to one's parents, to be loyal to friends, to fight without retreating, and to kill only when necessary. The *hwarang* lived by these principles which came to be known as the Law of the Hwarang (Hwarangdo). The principles were a blending of Buddhist, Confucian, Taoist and native concepts.

The *hwarang* took names based on historical and legendary Buddhist figures. They were devoted to the cult of the Maitreya, the Buddha of the Future, whom they hoped would bring about the unification of the three kingdoms of Koguryŏ, Paekche and Shilla under Shilla's rule. They made pilgrimages to sacred mountains and rivers to pray for the peace and prosperity of their nation by performing ceremonial songs and dances.

Kisaeng

Kisaeng were professional female entertainers who entertained with songs, dances and poetry recitation at feasts and banquets during the Chosŏn period (1392-1910). Members of the lowborn class *(ch'ŏnmin)*, they were selected for their beauty and trained at government institutes. They were taught reading, calligraphy, music, dance and other liberal arts. Some were also trained in medicine and martial arts.

Kisaeng were sent to provincial government offices to entertain guests and envoys from the capital and to border areas to entertain soldiers.

Two of the most famous *kisaeng* were Hwang Chin-i (early sixteenth century), who wrote poetry, and Non-gae (d. 1593), who, during the 1592-98 Japanese invasions, killed a Japanese general by jumping into the Namgang, a tributary of the Naktonggang River, while embracing him.

Korean Flag

The flag of Korea symbolizes much of the thought, philosophy and mysticism of the Orient. It is called *t'aegŭkki* in Korean; *t'aegŭk* being the name of the interlocked commas in the center, and *ki* being the word for flag.

Divided as it is into the blue *yin* and the red *yang* (*ŭm* and *yang* in Korean), the *t'aegŭk* represents the most fundamental cosmological and existential principle in Oriental philosophy. The two opposites, the negative, female principle *yin* and the positive, male principle *yang* express the dualism of the cosmos: fire and water, day and night, darkness and light, creation and destruction, and so forth. Thus the two commas turning together indicate that while there is constant movement within the sphere of infinity, there is also harmony.

The black bars at the corners of the flag are trigrams from the *I Ching (Book of Changes)*, an ancient Chinese book that developed the philosophy of *yin* and *yang* into a system for understanding all things. They also embody the idea of opposition and balance. The three unbroken bars in the upper left corner represent heaven and the three broken bars in the lower right corner represent earth. The bars in the lower left corner, two solid with a broken one in the middle, represent fire. And the bars in the upper right corner, two broken with a solid one in the middle, represent water.

Although the symbols on the flag are ancient, the flag itself is rather new. The idea of having a flag first arose in 1872 in treaty negotiations with Japan, which reproached Korea for firing on a Japanese boat whose flag was flying in clear view. Until that time, Koreans had never viewed flags as symbols of national sovereignty. The necessity of having a flag became more apparent as Korea began to have more and more contact with other nations. In 1882 a government mission sailing to Japan decided to make a flag to fly over their headquarters in Japan. They based their design on ideas that had been discussed and agreed upon before their departure.

Many variations of the design appeared thereafter, especially during the Japanese occupation when Korean flags were banned. The present standard—white with a blue and red *t'aegŭk* in the center and black trigrams in the corners—was established in 1948.

Kwagŏ

Civil examinations for appointment to public office were first instituted by Koryŏ in 957 and continued to be the method of appointment throughout the Chosŏn period (1392-1910). The examination system, called *kwagŏ,* was divided into two branches: civil and military. Only members of the *yangban* class (*see* entry in this chapter) could qualify to sit for the examinations and applications were restricted. Qualifying examinations were conducted at two levels, the lower or licentiate level (*sŏkwa* or *saengjin-gwa*) and the higher or erudite level (*taekwa* or *mun-gwa*). There were two licentiate examinations: the *saengwon-gwa* that tested the candidate's knowledge of the Four Books and Five Classics of China, and the *chinsakwa* that tested the candidate's skill in composing various Chinese literary forms. Candidates who passed one of these examinations might enter the national Confucian academy Sŏnggyun-gwan in Seoul (*see* Sŏnggyun-gwan in Famous Places and Monuments) and then sit for the erudite examination, which was also conducted in two stages. Candidates who passed the erudite examinations sat for the *chŏnshi,* an examination conducted in the presence of the king. Those who passed the palace examination were individually ranked and the highest ranking man was appointed to a middle level post.

The military examination was also conducted in three stages. It tested the candidate's skills in the military arts such as archery, lance, and horsemanship, and his knowledge of the Five Classics and various military texts.

In principle, the examinations were to be held every three years but special examinations were held from time to time to celebrate important events such as the accession of a new king.

March First Independence Movement

The Samil Undong, which took place on March 1, 1919, was a well-planned independence movement against the Japanese that was inspired by Woodrow Wilson's doctrine of self-determination of nations that stated that no people should be dominated by another people against their will. It was historically significant as it increased a spirit of national unity among Koreans and showed the world that Koreans did not desire to be ruled by Japan.

The planners, representatives of various independence organizations, most of which had some religious affiliation, intended the movement to be peaceful. They made well-organized plans and arrangements. These included the writing of a Declaration of Independence and sending copies of it to participants throughout the country.

The movement began with the promulgation of the Declaration of Independence and its public reading in Pagoda Park (*see* entry in Famous Places and Monuments) on March 1, or Sam-il in Korean, which was chosen to take advantage of the crowds of people converging on Seoul for the funeral of former King Kojong scheduled for March 3. At a pre-arranged signal, the declaration was also publicly read at over 1,500 places throughout the country. After the public reading of the declaration, the crowds marched in the streets shouting "Long live Korean independence!" and gradually demonstrations for independence spread to the countryside and eventually the whole country.

Though no armed revolt or violence was planned, the Government-General crushed the demonstrations with force, brutally killing thousands of people in the process. Many of the independence leaders and fighters were arrested and imprisoned and many fled the country and joined activist groups in exile.

In recognition of the historical significance of the Samil Undong, March 1 was made a national holiday in 1949.

Tripitaka Koreana

One of Korea's greatest treasures, the *Tripitaka Koreana (Koryŏ taejanggyŏng)* is the most comprehensive execution of the Buddhist canon, Tripitaka *(changgyŏng)*. It consists of 81,258 wooden printing blocks engraved on both sides. The blocks are 27 inches long, 10 inches wide, and 1 inch thick (69cm x 25cm x 2.5cm) and an average block has about 320 characters carved in reverse on each side. The blocks are divided into 1,512 books comprising 9 categories of texts, including sutras, scriptural commentaries, philosophical writings and disciplinary rules. There are also illustrations and decorations.

The task of creating this enormous canon and carving it on wooden printing blocks took 16 years, from 1236 to 1251. It was done by order of King Kojong (r. 1213-59) of Koryŏ to replace an earlier collection of blocks for printing Buddhist scriptures called *Ch'ojo changgyŏng* that had been burnt by Mongol invaders in 1232. The *Ch'ojo changgyŏng* had been created in fulfillment of a vow made by King Hyŏnjong (r. 1009-31) during the Khitan invasions in the early eleventh century that if the nation were spared he would place all of the known Buddhist scriptures on printing blocks in order to disseminate Buddhist thought. King Kojong vowed to recreate the collection in the hope Buddha would help expel the Mongol invaders.

The task was begun by a committee of scholarly monks led by monk Sugi, a noted scholar and linguist. They examined and compared various canonical collections to create their enormous canon which is the most complete corpus of Buddhist writings in East Asia.

The blocks for printing the canon were carved on the island of Kanghwado where the court had taken refuge from the Mongol invaders. The blocks were first housed in a building near the royal palace on Kanghwado, and later moved to Sŏnwonsa, a temple on the same island. During the early years of Chosŏn, the blocks were moved to Chijangsa Temple near Seoul. In 1399 they were moved to their present location, Haeinsa Temple, near Taegu.

The blocks are housed in a specially designed building, which is a marvel in itself. The ancient wooden building has vents which allow the mountain air to circulate around the blocks to ensure preservation.

Yangban

The members of the two orders of officialdom, civil officials and military officials, who served in the bureaucracy of the Chosŏn Kingdom (1392-1910) were the *yangban*. However, with time, the term came to be used for the class priviledged to hold civil and military posts in the bureaucracy, the aristocracy, or literati as it is more commonly called.

Chosŏn society was divided into four strict classes: the literati, the professional middle class (*chung-in;* clerks, astrologers, doctors, interpreters), the peasantry (*sangmin;* farmers, artisans, shopkeepers), and the lowborn (*ch'ŏnmin;* slaves, entertainers, butchers, shamans). The classes were largely hereditary as people married within their class and social mobility was practically nonexistent.

Yangban lived only among *yangban,* not side by side with people of other classes. In cities, there were areas where only *yangban* could reside and in the countryside they lived in separate villages.

Appointment to government posts depended on one's success in the government examinations called *kwagŏ* (*see* entry in this chapter).

Rulers of Korea's Ancient Kingdoms

Koguryŏ
(37 B.C.-A.D. 668)

1.	Tongmyŏng-wang (57{58?}-19 B.C.)	37 - 19 B.C.
2.	Yuri-wang (d. A.D. 18)	19 B.C.- A.D. 18
3.	Taemushin-wang (d. 44)	18 - 44
4.	Minjung-wang (d. 48)	44 - 48
5.	Mobon-wang (d. 53)	48 - 53
6.	T'aejo-wang (47-165)	53 - 146
7.	Ch'adae-wang (71-165)	146 - 165
8.	Shindae-wang (89-179)	165 - 179
9.	Kogukch'ŏn-wang (d.197)	179 - 197
10.	Sansang-wang (d. 227)	197 - 227
11.	Tongch'ŏn-wang (d. 248)	227 - 248
12.	Chunch'ŏn-wang (224-270)	248 - 270
13.	Sŏch'ŏn-wang (d. 292)	270 - 292
14.	Pongsang-wang (d. 300)	292 - 300
15.	Mich'ŏn-wang (d. 331)	300 - 331
16.	Kogugwon-wang (d. 371)	331 - 371
17.	Sosurim-wang (d. 384)	371 - 384
18.	Kogugyang-wang (d. 391)	384 - 391
19.	Kwanggaet'o-wang (375-413)	391 - 413
20.	Changsu-wang (394-491)	413 - 491
21.	Munja-wang (d. 519)	491 - 519
22.	Anjang-wang (d. 531)	519 - 531
23.	Anwon-wang (d. 545)	531 - 545
24.	Yangwon-wang (d. 559)	545 - 559
25.	P'yŏngwon-wang (d. 590)	559 - 590
26.	Yŏngyang-wang (d. 618)	590 - 618
27.	Yŏngnyu-wang (d. 642)	618 - 642
28.	Pojang-wang (d. 682)	642 - 668

Paekche
(18 B.C.-A.D. 660)

1. Onjo-wang (d. A.D. 28)	18 B.C.-A.D. 28
2. Taru-wang (d. 77)	28 - 77
3. Kiru-wang (d. 128)	77 - 128
4. Kaeru-wang (d. 166)	128 - 166
5. Ch'ogo-wang (d. 214)	166 - 214
6. Kusu-wang (d. 234)	214 - 234
7. Saban-wang	234
8. Koi-wang (d. 286)	234 - 286
9. Ch'aekkye-wang (d. 298)	286 - 298
10. Punsŏ-wang (d. 304)	298 - 304
11. Piryu-wang (d. 344)	304 - 344
12. Kye-wang (d. 346)	344 - 346
13. Kŭnch'ogo-wang (d. 375), Ch'ogo II	346 - 375
14. Kŭn-gusu-wang (d. 384), Kusu II	375 - 384
15. Ch'imnyuwang (d. 385)	384 - 385
16. Chinsa-wang (d. 392)	385 - 392
17. Ashin-wang (d. 405), *also* Ahwa- & Abang-wang	392 - 405
18. Chŏnji-wang (d. 420)	405 - 420
19. Kuishin-wang (d. 427)	420 - 427
20. Piyu-wang (d. 455)	427 - 455
21. Kaero-wang (d. 475)	455 - 475
22. Munju-wang (d. 477)	475 - 477
23. Samgŭn-wang (465-479)	477 - 479
24. Tongsŏng-wang (d. 501)	479 - 501
25. Muryŏng-wang (d. 523)	501 - 523
26. Sŏng-wang (d. 554)	523 - 554
27. Widŏk-wang (d. 598)	554 - 598
28. Hye-wang (d. 599)	598 - 599
29. Pŏp-wang (d. 600)	599 - 600
30. Mu-wang (d. 641)	600 - 641
31. Ŭija-wang (d. 660)	641 - 660

Shilla
(57 B.C.-A.D. 935)
(Shilla unified the three kingdoms in 668)

1. Pak Hyŏkkŏse (69 B.C.-A.D. 4)		57 B.C.-A.D. 4
2. Namhae-wang		4 - 24
3. Yuri-wang		24 - 57
4. T'alhae-wang (d. 80)		57 - 80
5. P'asa-wang (d. 112)		80 - 112
6. Chimwa-wang (d. 134)		112 - 134
7. Ilsŏng-wang (d. 154)		134 - 154
8. Adalla-wang		154 - 184
9. Pŏlhyu-wang (d. 196)		184 - 196
10. Naehae-wang		196 - 230
11. Chobun-wang (d. 247)		230 - 247
12. Ch'ŏmhae-wang (d. 261)		247 - 261
13. Mich'u-wang (d. 284)		262 - 284
14. Yurea-wang (d. 298)		284 - 298
15. Kirim-wang (289-310)		298 - 310
16. Hŭlhae-wang (d. 356)		310 - 356
17. Naemul-wang (d. 402)		356 - 402
18. Shilsŏng-wang (d. 417)		402 - 417
19. Nulji-wang (d. 458)		418 - 458
20. Chabi-wang (d. 479)		458 - 479
21. Soji-wang (d. 500)		479 - 500
22. Chijŭng-wang (437-514)		500 - 514
23. Pŏphŭng-wang (d. 540)		514 - 540
24. Chinhŭng-wang (534-576)		540 - 576
25. Chinji-wang (d. 579)		576 - 579
26. Chinp'yŏng-wang (d. 632)		579 - 632
27. Sŏndŏk-yŏwang (d. 647)		632 - 647
28. Chindŏk-yŏwang (d. 654)		647 - 654
29. T'aejong Muyŏl-wang (604-661)		654 - 661
30. Munmu-wang (d. 681)		661 - 681
31. Shinmun-wang (d. 692)		681 - 692
32. Hyoso-wang (643-702)		692 - 702

33. Sŏngdŏk-wang (d. 737)	702 - 737
34. Hyosŏng-wang (d. 742)	737 - 742
35. Kyŏngdŏk-wang (d. 765)	742 - 765
36. Hyegong-wang (756-780)	765 - 780
37. Sŏndŏk-wang (d. 785)	780 - 785
38. Wonsŏng-wang (d. 798)	785 - 798
39. Sosŏng-wang (d. 800)	798 - 800
40. Aejang-wang (788-809)	800 - 809
41. Hŏndŏk-wang (d. 826)	809 - 826
42. Hŭngdŏk-wang (d. 836)	826 - 836
43. Hŭigang-wang (d. 838)	836 - 838
44. Minae-wang (d. 839)	838 - 839
45. Shinmu-wang (d. 839)	839
46. Munsŏng-wang (d. 857)	839 - 857
47. Hŏnan-wang (d. 861)	857 - 861
48. Kyŏngmun-wang (d. 875)	861 - 875
49. Hŏn-gang-wang (d. 886)	875 - 886
50. Chŏnggang-wang (d. 887)	886 - 887
51. Chinsŏng-yŏwang (d. 897)	887 - 897
52. Hyogong-wang (d. 912)	897 - 912
53. Shindŏk-wang (d. 917)	912 - 917
54. Kyŏngmyŏng-wang (d. 924)	917 - 924
55. Kyŏng-ae-wang (d. 927)	924 - 927
56. Kyŏngsun-wang (d. 978)	927 - 935

Koryŏ
(918-1392)

1. T'aejo (877-943)	918 - 943
2. Hyejong (d. 945)	943 - 945
3. Chŏngjong (923-949)	945 - 949
4. Kwangjong (925-975)	949 - 975
5. Kyŏngjong (955-981)	975 - 981
6. Sŏngjong (960-997)	981 - 997
7. Mokchong (980-1009)	997 - 1009

8. Hyŏnjong (992-1031)	1009 - 1031
9. Tŏkchong (1016-1034)	1031 - 1034
10. Chŏngjong (1018-1046)	1034 - 1046
11. Munjong (1019-1083)	1046 - 1083
12. Sunjong (1046-1083)	1083
13. Sŏnjong (1049-1094)	1083 - 1094
14. Hŏnjong (1084-1097)	1094 - 1095
15. Sukchong (1054-1105)	1095 - 1105
16. Yejong (1079-1122)	1105 - 1122
17. Injong (1109-1146)	1122 - 1146
18. Ŭijong (1124-1170)	1146 - 1170
19. Myŏngjong (1131-1202)	1170 - 1197
20. Shinjong (1144-1204)	1197 - 1204
21. Hŭijong (1181-1237)	1204 - 1211
22. Kangjong (1152-1213)	1211 - 1213
23. Kojong (1192-1259)	1213 - 1259
24. Wonjong (1219-1274)	1259 - 1274
25. Ch'ungnyŏl-wang (1236-1308)	1274 - 1308
26. Ch'ungsŏn-wang (1275-1314)	1308 - 1313
27. Ch'ungsuk-wang (1294-1339)	1313 - 1330, 1332 - 1339
28. Ch'unghye-wang (1315-1344)	1330 - 1332, 1339 - 1344
29. Ch'ungmok-wang (1337-1348)	1344 - 1348
30. Ch'ungjŏng-wang (1337-1352)	1348 - 1351
31. Kongmin-wang (1330-1374)	1351 - 1374
32. U-wang (1364-1398)	1374 - 1388
33. Ch'ang-wang (1381-1389)	1388 - 1389
34. Kongyang-wang (1345-1394)	1389 - 1392

Chosŏn
(Yi Dynasty)
(1392-1910)

1. T'aejo (1335-1408)	1392 - 1398

2. Chŏngjong (1357-1419)   1392 - 1400
3. T'aejong (1367-1422)   1400 - 1418
4. Sejong-taewang, Sejong the Great (1397-1450)   1418 - 1450
5. Munjong (1414-1452)   1450 - 1452
6. Tanjong (1441-1457)   1452 - 1455
7. Sejo (1417-1468)   1455 - 1468
8. Yejong (1450-1469)   1468 - 1469
9. Sŏngjong (1457-1494)   1469 - 1494
10. Yŏnsan-gun (1476-1506)   1494 - 1506
11. Chungjong (1448-1544)   1506 - 1544
12. Injong (1515-1545)   1544 - 1545
13. Myŏngjong (1534-1567)   1545 - 1567
14. Sŏnjo (1552-1608)   1567 - 1608
15. Kwanghae-gun (1575-1641),   1608 - 1623
    dethroned & demoted
16. Injo (1595-1649)   1623 - 1649
17. Hyojong (1619-1659)   1649 - 1659
18. Hyŏnjong (1641-1674)   1659 - 1674
19. Sukchong (1661-1720)   1674 - 1720
20. Kyŏngjong (1688-1724)   1720 - 1724
21. Yŏngjo (1694-1776)   1724 - 1776
22. Chŏngjo (1752-1800)   1776 - 1800
23. Sunjo (1790-1834)   1800 - 1834
24. Hŏnjong (1827-1849)   1834 - 1849
25. Ch'ŏlchong (1831-1863)   1849 - 1863
26. Kojong (1852-1919)   1863 - 1907
27. Sunjong (1874-1926)   1907 - 1910

---

*The names which the Kings of Koryo and Choson are called today, (e.g., T'aejo, Sejong) are not the names they were Known by in life, but the names by which they were canonized posthumously. The names end in either jong and jo. Jong, meaning "clan," indicates that the king was a legitimate successor to the throne. Jo, meaning "progenitor," indicates that the king was not in the direct line of succession but acced to throne by a coup or some other means.

Bibliography

Arnold, Denis, ed. *The New Oxford Companion to Music*. Oxford: Oxford University Press, 1983, pp.1025-1031.

Adams, Edward B. *Focus on Korea*. Seoul: Seoul International Publishing House, 1986.

_____. *Palaces of Seoul*. Seoul: Seoul International Tourist Publishing Company, 1982.

Apa Productions. *Korea,* Insight Guides 6. Hong Kong: Apa Publications Ltd., 1981.

Asian Art Museum of San Francisco. *5000 Years of Korean Art*. Seoul: Samhwa Printing Co., 1979.

Chai, Ch'u and Winberg Chai. *Confucianism*. New York: Barron's Educational Series, Inc., 1973.

Chang Suk-in. *Modern Conversational Korean*. Seoul: Seoul Computer Press, 1982.

Cheong, Chae-hyok. "Hahn-yahk: Oriental Medicine," *Korea Quarterly,* Winter 1979, Vol.1 No.1, pp.12-19.

Clark, Charles Allen. *Religions of Old Korea*. Seoul: Christian Literature Society of Korea, 1961.

Clark, Donald N. and James H. Grayson. *Discovering Seoul*. Seoul: Royal Asiatic Society, 1986.

Covell, Jon Carter. *Korea's Cultural Roots*. Seoul: Hollym International Corp., 1982.

Crane, Paul S. *Korean Patterns*. Seoul: Royal Asiatic Society, 1978.

Cultural Properties Research Institute. *Cultural Properties Survey, Cultural Relics In and Around Seoul.* Seoul: Cultural Properties Research Institute, 1985.

_____. *Tanch'ong of Royal Tombs.* Seoul: Cultural Properties Research Institute, 1981.

Eckert, Carter J., *et al. Korea Old and New: A History.* Seoul: Ilchokak, 1990.

Goepper, Roger, *et al. Treasures from Korea.* London: Trustees of the British Museum, 1984.

Grant, Bruce K. *A Guide to Korean Characters.* Seoul: Hollym International Corp., 1979.

Grayson, James Huntley. *Korea A Religious History.* Oxford: Clarendon Press, 1989.

Handler, Sarah. "The Korean and Chinese Furniture Traditions," *Korean Culture,* Vol.5, No.2, June 1984, pp.4-19.

Han, Suzanne Crowder. *Korea.* Seoul: Hollym International Corp., 1986.

_____. *Kyongju.* Seoul: Hollym International Corp., 1988.

_____. *Seoul.* Seoul: Hollym International Corp., 1986.

Han, Woo-keun. *The History of Korea.* Seoul: Eul-Yoo Publishing Co., 1970.

Henthorn, William E. *A History of Korea.* New York: The Free Press, 1971.

Howard, Keith. *Bands, Songs, and Shamanistic Rituals.* Seoul: Royal Asiatic Society, 1990.

Hoyt, James. *Songs of the Dragons Flying to Heaven.* Seoul: Korean National Commission for UNESCO, 1971.

Huhm, Halla Pai. *Kut, Korean Shamanist Rituals.* Seoul: Hollym International Corporation, 1980.

Hyun, Peter. *Introducing Korea.* Seoul: Jungwoo-sa, 1979.

_____. *Koreana.* Seoul: Korea Britannica Corporation, 1984.

Ilyon. *Samguk Yusa.* Translated by Ha Tae-Hung and Grafton K. Mintz. Seoul: Yonsei University Press, 1986.

Janelli, Roger L. and Dawnhee Yim Janelli. *Ancestor Worship and Korean Society.* Stanford: Stanford University Press, 1982.

Joo, Nam-chull. "Buddhist Temple Architecture in Korea," *Koreana,* Vol. 3, No. 1, 1989.

Kendall, Laurel and Griffin Dix, eds. *Religion and Ritual in Korean Society.* Berkeley: Institute of East Asian Studies, University of California, 1987.

Kendall, Laurel and Mark Peterson, eds. *Korean Women: View from the Inner Room.* Cushing: East Rock Press, 1983.

Kim, Hee-jin. *The Art of Maedŭp.* Seoul: Koryo Sojok Corp., 1982.

Kim, Hyŏn-jun. *Sach'al, kŭsoge kitŭn ŭimi (Temple, the Pervading Meaning).* Seoul: Kyobo Mungo, 1991.

Kim, Ick-dal, pub. *Korea, Its People and Culture.* Seoul: Hakwon- sa, Ltd., 1970.

Kim, Jaihiun Joyce. *Master Sijo Poems from Korea.* Seoul: Si-sa-yong-o-sa Publishers, Inc.,1982.

Kim Jong-ki. *Seoul: Host City of the '88 Olympics.* Seoul: KBS

Enterprises, 1983.

Kim, Yong-hwan. *Genre Pictures of Korea.* Seoul: Minmungo, 1988.

Kim, Young-sook. *Korean Royal Costumes of the Late Chosŏn Period.* Seoul: Minjok Munhwa Mungo Co., Ltd., 1987.

Korea Buddhism Chogye Order. *Korea Buddhism.* Seoul: Korea Buddhism Chogye Order, 1986.

Korean National Commission for UNESCO. *Korean Folklore.* Seoul: Si-sa-yong-o-sa Publishers, Inc., 1983.

Korean Overseas Information Service. *Arts,* Korea Background Series, Vol. 8. Seoul: Korean Overseas Information Service, 1982.

_____. *Customs and Traditions,* Korea Background Series, Vol. 10. Seoul: Korean Overseas Information Service, 1982.

_____. *A Handbook of Korea.* Seoul: Seoul International Publishing House, 1987.

_____. *Korean Art Guide.* Seoul: Yekyong Publications Co., Ltd., 1987.

_____. *Korean Craftsmen on Parade.* Seoul: Korean Overseas Information Service, 1982.

_____. *Traditional Korean Crafts Exhibition.* Seoul: Korean Overseas Information Service, 1982.

Kusan Sunim. *The Way of Korean Zen.* Translated by Martine Fages. New York: Weatherhill, 1985.

Lee, Ki-baik. *A New History of Korea.* Translated by Edward W. Wagner with Edward J. Shultz. Seoul: Ilchokak, 1984.

Lee, Kyong-hee. "Virtuous Saimdang excelled in arts," *Korea Herald,* October 18, 1991, p.12.

Lee, Peter H. *Anthology of Korean Literature.* Honolulu: University Press of Hawaii, 1981.

McCune, Evelyn B. *The Inner Art: Korean Screens.* Seoul: Po Chin Chai Co., Ltd., 1983.

Medley, Margaret. *A Handbook of Chinese Art.* New York: Harper and Row, 1964.

Moes, Robert. *Auspicious Spirits.* Washington: International Exhibitions Foundation, 1983.

_____. *Korean Art from the Brooklyn Museum.* New York: Universe Books, 1987.

National Museum of Korea. *Beauty of Korea: Traditional Costumes, Ornaments and Cloth Wrappings.* Seoul: National Museum of Korea, 1988.

The New Encyclopedia Britannica, Vol. 17 Macropaedia. Chicago: Encyclopedia Britannica, Inc., 1991, pp. 745-747.

Osgood, Cornelius. *The Koreans and Their Culture.* New York: The Ronald Press Company, 1951.

Pak, Ki-hyuk with Sydney D. Gamble. *The Changing Korean Village.* Seoul: Shin-hung Press, 1975.

Palmer, Spenser J. *Confucian Rituals in Korea.* Seoul: Po Chin Lai, Ltd, 1986.

Pratt, Keith. *Korean Music: Its History and Its Performance.* Seoul: Jung Eum Sa Publishing Corporation, 1987.

Randel, Don Michael, ed. *The New Harvard Dictionary of Music.*

Cambridge: The Belknap Press of Harvard University, 1986, pp. 257-259.

Rector, Gary. "Our Flags and Their Symbolism," *Friendship*, Vol. 14, No. 2, 1987.

Rice, Edward. *Eastern Definitions*. Garden City: Anchor Books, 1980.

Rutt, Richard. *James Scarth Gale and His History of the Korean People*. Seoul: Royal Asiatic Society, 1972.

Saccone, Richard. "Shin saimdang represents model woman of Yi Dynasty," *Korea Herald*, May 21, 1992, p. 7.

Sadie, Stanley, ed. *The New Grove Dictionary of Music and Musicians*, Vol.10. London: Macmillan Publishers, Ltd.,1980, pp.192-208.

Seoul Metropolitan Government. *Seoul Then and Now*. Seoul: Seoul Metropolitan Government, 1984.

Shin, Young-hoon. "The Function and Beauty of the Traditional Korean House," *Koreana*, Vol. 2, No. 4, 1989, pp. 4-13.

Song, Bang-song. *Korean Music and Instruments*. Seoul: National Classical Music Institute, 1979.

Sym, Myung-Ho. *The Making of Modern Korean Poetry: Foreign Influences and Native Creativity*. Seoul: Seoul National University Press, 1982.

Williams, C. A. S. *Outlines of Chinese Symbolism and Art Motives*. New York: Dover Publications, 1976.

Yarfitz, Denise. "Traditional Korean Games," *Korean Culture*, Vol. 5, No. 1, March 1984, pp.16-27.

Yoon, Se-yeong. "Independence Fighter An Chung-Gŭn," *Seoul,* April 1986, pp. 18-22.

Yoo, Yushin. *Korea the Beautiful: Treasures of the Hermit Kingdom.* Carson: Golden Pond Press, 1987.

Yoon, Bok-cha, *et al. Korean Furniture and Culture.* Seoul: Shinkwang Publishing Co., 1988.

Zong, In-sob. *An Introduction to Korean Literature.* Seoul: Hyangnin-Sa, 1970.

Zozayong. *Guardians of Happiness.* Seoul: Emileh Museum, 1982.

Glossary

a-ak: Court music, also called *chong-ak*

ajaeng: A long bowed zither

Amit'a bul: Amitahba, the Buddha of Infinite Light, the ruler of the Pure Land, or Western Paradise as it is sometimes called.

anae: Also *an saram*, "one inside," a term by which a man refers to his wife.

Ananda: Korean for Ananda, the cousin and personal attendant of Sakyamuni, the historical Buddha

anbang: The main room of the women's quarters (*anch'ae*) of a traditional upper-class Korean house

anch'ae: The women's quarters of a traditional Korean upper-class house

aniri: The recitative portions of a *p'ansori* performance

anju: Foods eaten with liquor

an saram: Also *anae*, "one inside," a term by which a man refers to his wife.

chabara: Thin circular brass cymbals also known as *para*, *chegŭm*, *tongbal*, *hyangbal*, *yobal*, and *pal*.

chagae: Lacquerware inlaid with mother-of-pearl

chagŭnjip: "Little house," the term by which family members refer to the home of uncles other than the oldest uncle.

ch'ajŏnnori: A game usually played at New Year's and also called *tongch'aessaum*, it is a mock battle between two teams wielding giant A-frames, the object being to make the tip of the opponent's A-frame touch the ground.

changdoktae: Terrace where sauce jars are stored

changga kada: A phrase used to refer to a man getting married

changgi: A variation of an ancient prototype of chess, this board game is a war between two camps of men, the object being to capture the opponent's king.

changgo: The chief percussion instrument of Korea, this two-headed drum shaped like an hourglass is known by a variety of names—*sŏlchanggo* in farmer's music and dance, *seyogo* in historical sources and *changgu* in central Korea

ch'anggŭk: A folk opera employing *p'ansori* artists that developed from *p'ansori* around the beginning of the twentieth century

changgunshin: The General God, a shamanic deity

changja: First son

changmyŏngga: Professional name maker

changrye: Funeral

Changsa: Super Strong Man, the title given to the winner of a *ssirŭm* (Korean wrestling) match

changsŭng: The common name for the spirit posts that stand, usually in pairs, at the entrances to villages and temples and whose function is to protect the area from evil spirits and thereby ensure the peace and prosperity of those who reside therein.

ch'arye: A Confucian ritual to pay homage to ancestors of four generations back performed in the morning on certain traditional holidays.

ch'arye sang: The table of food offered to ancestors in Confucian rites performed in the morning on certain traditional holidays.

chegi: A shuttlecock used in a kicking game that is called by the same name; it is kicked with the instep of the foot.

chegŭm: Another name for *chabara*, brass cymbals

chehyang: The collective name for the Confucian rites performed at the royal ancestral shrine Chongmyo to honor Yi Dynasty royalty.

cherye-ak: Music performed for rituals

chesa: The collective name for the Confucian rituals through which Koreans pay homage to their ancestors

chi: A short transverse bamboo flute with a mouthpiece

chiap: Pressure point massage

chibang: The tangible object of veneration in *kije* and *ch'arye* ancestral rites, it is a piece of paper bearing the name, title and place of origin of the ancestor or ancestors honored in the rites. It is burned at the end of the rites.

Chiguk ch'ŏnwang: Dhrtarastra, the Guardian of the East, one of the Lokapala (Sach'ŏnwang), the Four Heavenly Kings that protect Buddhist temples

Chijang posal: The Buddhist deity Ksitigarba, the Bodhisattva of Hell

Ch'ilsŏng: The Big Dipper, the Seven Star Spirit of Taoism and Shamanism

Ch'ilsŏk: The seventh day of the seventh lunar month

ch'im: Acupuncture

ch'ima: Skirt

ching: A large, flat, lipped bronze gong also called *taegŭm, kŭm, na,* and *kŭmna*; to play, it is held in one hand and struck with a mallet.

chin-go: A barrel drum supported on a four-legged wooden stand, it is the largest Korean drum in current use.

chinsakwa: Part of the licentiate level examination (*sŏkwa* or *saengjingwa*) that was part of the *kwagŏ* examination for appointment to public office, it tested the candidate's skill in composing various Chinese literary forms.

Chiphyŏnjŏn: Hall of Worthies, an institute established by King Sejong (r. 1418-50) for the accumulation and dissemination of knowledge useful to government and to the populace.

Chip'yŏng yŏram (*Exemplar for Efficient Government*): The first manual for government administrators, it was compiled in 1441 to provide guidance for officials in the form of selections from administrative failures and achievements in the past.

Chishin: The Foundation God, the Shamanist deity that resides in the foundation of a house

cho: Millet

Ch'obok: The eighth day of the sixth lunar month; one of three days collectively known as Pok-nal that are thought to be the hottest times of the year

ch'ogajip: Thatched house

Chogye-jong: The predominant form of Buddhism in Korea, it emphasizes constant discipline, prayer, the study of sutras and meditation.

chŏgori: The bolero—and vest-like garments of the women's and men's traditional two-piece Korean costume called *hanbok*

chŏk: End-blown notched bamboo flute

chokpo: The genealogical table that traces one's lineage back to the progenitor of one's clan.

chŏl: Buddhist temple

chŏlchin: Palpation of the pulse and stomach for diagnostic purposes

chŏlgo: A barrel drum mounted at a slant in a wooden stand

chŏmjangi: Fortuneteller

chŏnsŏ: An ornate style of calligraphic writing

Ch'ŏndogyo: First founded as Tonghak (Eastern Learning), the Religion of the Heavenly Way teaches that its god, Hanullim, is to be discovered within oneself and that Hanullim and humans are not separate beings but are one.

ch'ŏng: The color blue

chŏng-ak: Court music, also called *a-ak*

ch'ŏngja: Porcelaneous stoneware with a fine bluish-green glaze known in the West by the French term celadon

chongmyo-ak: Ritual music played to accompany Confucian rites performed at Chongmyo, the royal ancestral shrine of the Yi Dynasty, to venerate the kings and queens of the Chosŏn Kingdom (1392-1910)

chŏngt'o: Korean for Pure Land

chŏngjagak: A building for conducting the ritual sacrifices at a tomb

ch'ŏnmin: The lowborn (slaves, entertainers, butchers, shamans), one of four classes into which Chosŏn society was strictly divided

chŏnshi: An examination (*kwagŏ*) conducted in the presence of the king

Ch'ŏnshin: The Heavenly God, a major shamanic deity

Ch'opail: Literally meaning "eighth day of the month," it is Buddha's birthday, the eighth day of the fourth lunar month.

chorach'i: Also known as *kyŏngnaech'wi*, a band that accompanies Buddhist dances that are performed during certain Buddhist rites

chosang: Ancestors

ch'osŏ: A cursive style of calligraphic writing known as "running grass."

chotkarak: Chopsticks

Chowang: The Kitchen God, the shamanic deity that resides in the kitchen

ch'uimsae: Calls of encouragement made by a drummer at appropriate phrase endings in a *p'ansori* performance

Chujahak: The Korean term for the Neo-Confucian philosophy of Chu Hsi

ch'uk: A large percussion idiophone consisting of a wooden box and a round wooden hammer, it functions solely as part of a starting signal for ritual music and is also called *kang*.

chuldarigi: A large scale tug of war game usually staged during the New Year's season

Chungbok: The eighteenth day of the sixth lunar month; one of three days collectively known as Pok-nal that are thought to be the hottest times of the year.

Chungch'ujol: Literally "mid autumn day," another name for Ch'usŏk, the Harvest Moon Festival, a time of thanksgiving celebrated on the fifteenth day of the eighth lunar month.

chung-in: The professional middle class (clerks, astrologers, doctors, interpreters), one of four classes into which Chosŏn society was strictly divided

Chŭngjang ch'ŏnwang: Virudhaka, the Guardian of the South, one of the Lokapala (Sach'ŏnwang), the Four Heavenly Kings that protect Buddhist temples

chungmae: The arranged meeting of a man and a woman through a go-between or matchmaker for the purpose of marriage

churye: The master of ceremonies at a wedding

Ch'usŏk: Harvest Moon Festival, a time of thanksgiving celebrated on the fifteenth day of the eighth lunar month; also called Chungch'ujŏl, meaning "mid autumn day," and Han-gawi, the meaning and origin of which is unclear

chwado kut: A style of farmer's music and dance (*nong-ak*) performed in the eastern half of the country and the inland areas of Chŏlla-do.

chwago: A medium-size barrel drum hung vertically in a wooden frame, used mainly in court and aristocratic music

haesŏ: A square style of calligraphic writing

haegŭm: A 2-string spike fiddle, known onomatopoeically as *kkangkkang-i*, used in various musical genres

haengsŏ: A semicursive style of calligraphic writing

haengnangch'ae: The servants quarters in a traditional upper-class

Korean house

haet'ae: A stone fire-eating beast

ham: A box of bridal gifts the groom's family sends to the home of the bride's family.

Ham saseyo!: "Box for sale!"; a phrase the bearers of a *ham*, a box of bridal gifts, call out as they approach the bride's home.

Hananim: The shamanistic deity, the Lord of Heaven, the Celestial Emperor of the Heavenly Kingdom, who rules over all the spirits

hanbang: Meaning "Korean prescription," this term has come to be used for a variety of traditional healing techniques.

hanbok: The traditional two-piece Korean costume comprising a bolero-like top and long wrap skirt for women and a vest-like jacket and blousy pants for men.

hang-ari: A ceramic storage jar also known as *onggi* and *tok* and by the English generic name *kimch'i* pot.

Han-gawi: Harvest Moon Festival, also called Ch'usŏk, a thanksgiving celebrated on the fifteenth day of the eighth lunar month

hangnyŏl: Also called *tollimja*, it is one of the characters of a given name that indicates the bearer's generation.

han-gŭl: The Korean alphabet that consists of twenty-four letters—fourteen consonants, and ten vowels—and is often called *ka-na-da* using the first three syllables of the alphabet.

hanja: The Korean term for Chinese characters

hanji: A term, literally meaning "Korean paper," generally used for paper made of mulberry pulp.

Hanshik: Cold Food Day, the one hundred fifth day after the Winter Solstice (T'ongji), when Koreans clean the graves of their forebears and perform ancestral rites and, as the name implies, eat cold food.

Hanul: The triunal god of the indigenous Korean religion Taejonggyo

Hanullim: The god worshiped in Ch'ŏndogyo, an indigenous Korean religion first founded in 1860 under the name Tonghak

hanyak: Herbal medicine

harubang: The name by which spirit posts are known on Chejudo Island.

ho: A sobriquet, it is generally made up of two very expressive Chinese characters chosen to symbolize one's self-image, creed, ideals and aspirations.

hŏn-ga: The ground orchestra, one of two orchestras that perform antiphonally to perform Confucian shrine music and royal ancestral shrine music

hongsalmun: A red arrow gate that stands in front of a tomb and near the shrine of a *hyanggyo* or *sŏwon* to indicate a sacred enclosure

hun: A globular vessel flute made of clay that is used in musical ensembles that accompany rites to Confucius.

hunmin chŏng-ŭm: Meaning "correct sounds for teaching the people," the name under which the Korean alphabet, *han-gŭl*, was promulgated by King Sejong (r. 1418-1450) in October 1446.

hwach'ŏng: The singing of Buddhist chants

hwagak: A decorating technique using back-painted ox horn; *hwa* means "pictures" or "lustrous" and *gak* means "horn."

hwan-gap: The sixtieth birthday

hwarang: A troop of young warriors, usually in their mid teens, organized to supplement the elite units that formed the core of Shilla's military forces.

Hwarangdo: The Law of the Hwarang, the principles the *hwarang*, a troop of young warriors during Shilla, lived by.

hwat'u: A deck of 48 plastic matchbook-size cards—12 suits of 4 cards, each suit named for a month—used to play a variety of card games of varying complexity and also used for fortunetelling.

hyang-ak: Meaning "native music," the term refers to court music of early Korean origin, Chinese music that came to Korea before the T'ang Dynasty (618-906) and compositions of the Koryŏ (918-1392) and Chosŏn (1392-1910) periods.

hyangbal: Small cymbals (*chabara*) fastened to the thumb and middle finger and used like castanets by dancers.

hyangch'al: A system of using Chinese to write Korean that was used before the Korean alphabet (*han-gŭl*) was invented.

hyangga: The term for the poetry of the Shilla and early Koryŏ periods written in Korean by means of Chinese characters

hyanggyo: A local public institute that also functioned as a Confucian shrine during the Koryŏ (918-1392) and Chosŏn (1392-1910) periods. Each county had one.

idu: A writing system using Chinese characters phonetically for Korean grammatical endings and inflections that was used before the invention of the Korean alphabet (*han-gŭl*) in 1446.

ilchumun: The gate that leads into the grounds of a Buddhist temple and usually bears the name of the temple.

ilmu: The line dances performed during Confucian ceremonies.

Imjin woeran: The Korean name for the 1592-98 Japanese invasions of Korea which were led by warlord Toyotomi Hideyoshi.

in-gam tojang: A seal or chop bearing one's name that is registered with the government so that authenticity can be proven.

insam: Ginseng

Ipch'un: The onset of spring according to the lunar calendar

irŭm: The Korean term for name

kagok: A lengthy song cycle sung as a solo or duet with the accompaniment of a chamber ensemble.

ka-na-da: The first three syllables of the Korean alphabet, *han-gŭl*, it is the name by which the alphabet is often called.

Kanggangsuwollae: A circle dance performed by women in the southwestern part of Korea.

kasa: A long descriptive, and often episodic, narrative in poetic form characterized by extended use of parallelism.

kasa: A long narrative song in strophic or through-composed form; the singer switches back and forth between normal voice and falsetto

Kasŏp: Korean for Kasyatpa, a leading disciple of the Buddha

kayagŭm: Also called *kayatgo*, a long 12-string zither invented in the sixth century in Kaya, a tribal league that existed in the southern part of the Korean Peninsula

ki: A force or energy that circulates through the body.

kije: A Confucian ritual traditionally performed at midnight on the eve of the anniversary of an ancestor's death.

kimch'i: A pungent, fermented staple dish generally comprising cabbage or turnip seasoned with salt, green onions, garlic, ginger, red pepper, and shellfish.

kimjang kimch'i: Kimch'i made to eat throughout the winter.

kisaeng: A professional female entertainer who entertained with songs, dances and poetry recitation at feasts and banquets during the Chosŏn period (1392-1910)

kkokkal: Paper flowered hats worn by some of the performers of the *udo kut* style of farmer's music and dance (*nong-ak*).

kkwaenggwari: A small, lipped flat bronze gong chiefly used in farmer's music and dance (*nong-ak*), it is also called *kkaengmagi* and *soe* meaning "metal" and *sogŭm* meaning "small gong."

kŏbuk: Tortoise

kŏbuk nori: Tortoise game, a game (*nori*) in which two men, covered with a shell made of straw or corn husks, are driven on their hands and knees from house to house throughout a village to entertain and be entertained in return; the "tortoise" dances and performs antics and then the group is treated to food and drink.

kŏbuksŏn: Meaning "turtle ship," an ironclad battleship most famous for being used to defeat a Japanese armada during the 1592-98 Japanese invasions of Korea

koch'wi: Music that was played for royal processions

kohŭi: "Old and rare"; the seventieth birthday

kŏmun-go: A 6-string zither plucked with a stick, it was invented in Koguryŏ in the sixth century and is played mainly in court and folk ensembles.

konggi: A game, similar to the Western game jacks, traditionally played with small round stones, called *konggi*, but nowadays played with mass produced plastic and rubber *konggi*.

Kongja: The Korean name for Confucius

Koryŏ taejanggyŏng: The *Tripitaka Koreana*—81,258 wooden printing blocks, engraved on both sides, for printing the Buddhist canon, Tripitaka—the most complete corpus of Buddhist writings in East Asia

kosa: Simple shamanic rituals performed to secure the good offices of the household gods

kossaum: A large-scale, fast-paced pushing game played with two giant loop-like rope structures, the object being to push the other team's rope head to the ground

kug-ak: Korean classical music

kuk: Soup

kŭm: 7-string zither

Kŭmgang shinjang: Vajras, fierce-looking guardians painted in pairs on the doors of Buddhist temple gates to prevent evil spirits from entering the temple

kŭmjul: "Forbidding rope"; a straw rope hung across the gate to a house to announce the birth of a child; woven with pine branches, charcoal and red pepper to indicate a male, and with pine branches and charcoal to indicate a female

kunghap: A divination, for purposes of marriage, to determine if a man and woman would be a harmonious match

kungmun: A name by which the Korean alphabet (*han-gŭl*) was once called

Kŭngnakchŏn: The Korean name by which the main hall of a Buddhist temple is called if it contains an image of Amitahba, the Buddha of Infinite Light. *See* Taeungbojŏn and Taeungjŏn.

kunggwol: Palace

k'ŭnjip: "Big house"; the oldest son's household

kwagŏ: A system of examination for appointment to public office that was first instituted by Koryŏ in 957 and continued to be the method of appointment throughout the Chosŏn period (1392-1910). During Chosŏn, only members of the *yangban* class could qualify to sit for the exam.

kwangdae: A generic term for itinerant professional entertainers which included artists of masked dance drama, puppet plays, acrobatics, *p'ansori* and *sanjo*

Kwangmok ch'ŏnwang: Virupaska, the Guardian of the West, one of the Lokapala (Sach'ŏnwang), the Four Heavenly Kings that guard the cardinal points to protect the Buddhist world

Kwanseŭm posal: The Buddhist deity Avalokitsevara, the Bodhisattva of Mercy

kwibalki sul: Meaning "wine that sharpens the ears," this is wine traditionally drunk on the morning of Taeborŭm, the fifteenth day of the first lunar month, in the belief it will make the ears sharp and they will hear good news.

kyŏngnaech'wi: see *chorach'i*

maedŭp: The Korean word for knot, it is a generic term for a wide assortment of ornamental knot creations.

Malbok: The ninth day of the seventh lunar month; one of three days collectively known as Pok-nal that are thought to be the hottest times of the year

manshin: A shaman, a person who mediates between this world and the spiritual world to dissolve conflicts and tensions that are believed to exist between the dead and the living by reconciling the two

Mawang: Korean for the Buddhist term Mara, negative or demonic influences often depicted in a personified form as the demon Mara

minsog-ak: Folk music, also called *sog-ak*

minyo: Folk songs

Mirŭk bul: The Buddhist deity Maitreya, the coming or future Buddha

mokt'ak: A hand-held slit wooden drum used only by Buddhist monks to accompany sutra chanting

mudang: The vulgar term for a shaman, *manshin*

mumu: Also called *ilmu*, the military dance that is performed during Confucian ceremonies.

mun-gwa: Also called *taekwa*, the higher or erudite level examination that was part of the *kwagŏ*, the examination for appointment to public office which was first iustituted Koryŏ in 957 and continued throughout the Chosŏn Period (1382-1910)

munjin: Listening to the sound of a person's voice, one of four methods of physical examination used in traditional healing

munjin: Questioning a person about his medical history and symptoms, one of four methods of physical examination used in traditional healing

munmu: Also called *ilmu*, the civil dance that is performed during Confucian ceremonies.

munmyo-ak: Musical accompaniment for Confucian rites performed at Munmyo, the Temple of Confucius

Munsu posal: The Buddhist deity Manjusri, the Bodhisattva of Wisdom

Musok: Shamanism, the belief that every object in the natural world has a spirit.

myo: Grave

myoje: A grave-side Confucian ritual to pay homage to ancestors

Myŏngbujŏn: The Korean name of the hall in a Buddhist temple where Ksitigarba (Chijang posal), the Bodhisattva of Hell, is enshrined and where funerals are held.

myŏngdang: In geomancy, the points where the earth's energy is stored and flows; such points are considered propitious sites, especially for graves.

nabal: A long brass trumpet with no finger-holes played exclusively for processional music.

nabich'um: Butterfly Dance, a Buddhist prayer dance

nagak: A conch shell horn, also called n*a* and *sora*, used now exclusively in ensembles for processional music.

Nahan: Arhat, a disciple of Buddha, an enlightened being, usually depicted in groups of 16, 18 or 500

nodo: Double twirling drum performed only in *chongmyo-ak* and *munmyo-ak* ritual music

nogo: Crossed barrel drums used in *chongmyo-ak* and *munmyo-ak* ritual music

nŏlttwigi: A traditional jumping game similar to see-sawing played by girls and young women; two people play at a time by jumping at either end of the board (*nŏl*), as one returns to the board, the other is propelled into the air

nong-ak: Literally meaning "farm music," the music performed by a percussion band that plays and dances simultaneously

Nongsa chiksŏl (*Straight Talk on Farming*): A manual compiled under King Sejong (r. 1418-50) to meet the specific conditions of Korean agriculture.

nori: Game

norigae: A harmonious blend of knots, jewels, and tassels which women wore, and many still do, to embellish the simple lines of the traditional Korean dress.

nottari palki: Princess Bridge, a women's game dating from the fourteenth century generally played on the fifteenth day of the first lunar month; the players form a bridge of bended backs and a "princess," assisted by attendants, walks across the bridge, joins the line and another "princess" walks across and another so that the bridge not only perpetuates but also moves.

numaru: A spacious veranda-like elevated wooden floor with low wooden railings.

nŭng: A royal tomb

ŏ: A wooden tiger-shaped scraper played in *chongmyo-ak* and *munmyo-ak* ritual music to give a stopping signal

Obang Shinjang: The Five Direction Forces residing in every room and stall or pen within the walls or fences of a house

ogokpap: Meaning "five-grain rice," glutinous rice cooked together with millet, red beans, sorghum, and large beans, traditionally eaten on Taeborŭm, the fifteenth day of the first lunar moon

ohaeng: The Five Elements—fire, water, wood, metal and earth—which, according to Oriental philosophy, everything in the universe is derived from.

ondol: A system of heating the floor using under-the-floor flues to carry warm air from a central source of heat such as a kitchen fire, or an outside fire.

onggi: A ceramic storage jar, also known as *hang-ari* and *tok*

ongsŏng: A feature of gates of the Koryŏ period (918-1392), a semicircular fortifying wall extending beyond the entranceway of large gates that enabled defenders to attack invaders on several sides

paduk: A board game, known in the West by its Japanese name, *go*, that is a contest of wits between two players, one using black button-like markers and one using white, the object being to occupy more territory on the board than one's opponent.

paegil: The one hundredth day of a child's birth

paekcha: The white porcelain wares that were made throughout the Chosŏn period (1392-1910).

Paekchung: During Shilla (57 B.C.-A.D. 935) and Koryŏ (918-1392), the fifteenth day of the seventh lunar month when servants could transcend their social status by proving their physical prowess in wrestling (*ssirŭm*) matches

paem sul: Snake wine, commonly taken as a health rejuvenator

paem t'ang: Snake soup, commonly taken as a health rejuvenator

paji: Pants

pak: A fan-shaped wooden clapper played by the director of an ensemble to give a starting signal and a stopping signal

pakkat saram: Meaning "outside person," the term by which a woman refers to her husband

p'alcha: Four pairs of cyclical characters associated with one's *saju*, the year, month, day and hour of one's birth

pallim: The body expressions exhibited in a *p'ansori* performance

Palsangdo (*Eight Paintings from Sakyamuni's Life*): Eight paintings that present Buddha's birth in the Lumbini Gardens, his childhood bath in the fire of nine dragons, his meditation in the mountains, his struggles with Mara, the devil, his enlightenment under the Boddhi tree, scenes of him teaching, his death, and his passage into Nirvana.

P'alto chiri chi (*A Geographical Description of the Eight Provinces*): Compiled in 1432, a collection of information deemed essential to the governing of the country, such as administrative history of local governments, topographical features, checkpoints, fortifications, land area, population, native products, roads, garrisons, beacon communication sites, tombs, surnames and historical personages.

panch'an: Side dishes of food that round out a meal

p'ansori: A narrative, epic, dramatic folk vocal art form performed by one singer accompanied by one drummer playing one drum.

pap: Cooked rice

para: Large brass cymbals, or *chabara*, used mainly in Buddhist ceremonial dances, military processional music and shamanistic rituals.

parach'um: Buddhist cymbal dance performed during certain rites

pigak: A pavilion housing a *pisŏk*, a stone monument or stele

pinyŏ: A long pin thrust through the knotted hair of a woman as both a fastener and a decoration

pip'a: A pear-shaped, short-necked plucked fiddle introduced to Korea from Central Asia; a major string instrument during the Unified Shilla period, it is no longer used

p'iri: A cylindrically bored double reed oboe-like instrument made of bamboo

Pirojanabul: The Buddhist deity Vairocana, the Spreading the Light of Buddhist Truth Buddha

pisŏk: Stone monument or stele

Pohyŏn posal: The Buddhist deity Samantabhadra, the Bodhisattva of Power and Love, often depicted riding an elephant

pojagi: Wrapping cloths and covers traditionally used for wrapping clothes, bedding, precious objects, etc., to store and protect them from dust and to cover tables and trays of food to protect them from insects; also called *po*, *pok*, *poja*, and *pojaegi*.

Pok-nal: Three days of the lunar calendar collectively known as Pok-nal that are thought to be the three hottest times of the year when it is customary to try to beat the heat by eating various foods that are considered to be health rejuvenators.

pŏksu: The name by which spirit posts (*changsŭng*) are known in the Kyŏngsang-do and Chŏlla-do provinces.

pon: Place of origin

pŏpko: A large barrel drum set aslant on a four-legged wooden stand, played by two players, one at each end of the drum, who strike both drumheads and the body of the drum.

pŏpkoch'um: Buddhist dance in which the tribulations of the dead are symbolically relieved by the beating of a large barrel drum

pori: Bodhi, Enlightenment, the complete and perfect state experienced by the Buddha

posal: A Bodhisattva, a being destined to attain Buddhahood after countless rebirths, but delays the final act to assist others in their quest for salvation

poshin t'ang: Dog meat soup commonly taken as a health rejuvenator.

pu: Clay jar musical instrument played only in *munmyo-ak* ritual music

puch'ŏ: A Buddha

Puch'ŏnim oshinnal: Literally meaning "the Day Buddha came," Buddha's birthday is celebrated the eighth day of the fourth lunar month and is also called Ch'op'ail.

pudo: Korean for stupa, a memorial constructed over the relics of the Buddha or other important persons; also called *sungt'ap*

pujŏk: Talisman

puk: A shallow double-headed barrel drum with a wooden body; one head is struck with the palm of the left hand and the other head is struck with a stick held in the right hand

pulgyo: Buddhism

punch'ŏng: The predominant ceramic ware from around 1392 until the 1590s characterized by an overall white slip decoration

p'ung: Wind

p'ungsu: Geomancy; the term literally means "wind and water"

p'yebaek: A traditional ceremony following the marriage ceremony in which the bride and groom formally present themselves to the groom's parents to receive their blessings.

pyŏngp'ung: Literally meaning "windbreak," this is a highly decorated folding screen traditionally used to block drafts and at the same time enhance the interior of the home.

p'yŏn-gyŏng: A set of L-shaped chimes used for various pieces of music, most notably *munmyo-ak* and *chongmyo-ak*.

p'yŏnjong: A set of bronze bells used in various pieces of music, most notably *munmyo-ak* and *chongmyo-ak*.

Pyŏnso Kakssi: The Toilet Maid, the shamanistic spirit who resides in the toilet

Sach'ŏnwang: The Buddhist Lokapala, the Four Heavenly Kings, the rulers of the the four cardinal points that protect the Buddhist world

sadang: An ancestral shrine containing memorial tablets

saengjingwa: Also called *sokwa*, the lower or licentiate level examination that was part of the *kwagŏ*, the examination for appointment to government office during the Chosŏn period (1392-1910).

saengwongwa: Part of the licentiate level examination (*sokwa* or *saengjingwa*), which was part of the *kwagŏ* examination for appointment to public office, it tested the candidate's knowledge of the Four Books and Five Classics of China.

sagunja: The Four Noble Gentlemen—plum, orchid, chrysanthemum and bamboo—a popular motif of literati painting *saju*: The year, month, day, and hour of one's birth

saju p'alcha: A method of fortunetelling based on one's *saju*, the year, month, day, and hour of one's birth, and one's *p'alcha*, four pairs of cyclical characters associated with one's saju.

sambe: Bleached hemp cloth

Samguk sagi (*History of the Three Kingdoms*): The oldest extant Korean history, it was compiled in 1145 by a high government official named Kim Pu-shik.

Samguk yusa (*Memorabilia of the Three Kingdoms*): A collection of Buddhist lore, usually classed as a history because of its immeasurable importance to Korean historiography, written in the late thirteenth century by a Buddhist monk named Iryŏn.

samgye t'ang: A spring chicken stuffed with ginseng, jujubes, chestnuts and glutinous rice and cooked several hours in its own broth; a very popular dish considered a health rejuvenator.

Samonim: A title, meaning "teacher's wife," which is used to show respect when addressing a married woman.

Samshin-gak: A hall in a Buddhist temple dedicated to the Seven Star Spirit (Ch'ilsŏng), the Mountain Spirit (Sanshin), and the Lonely Saint (Toksŏng), three deities that derive from Taoism and Shamanism.

Samshin Halmŏni: Birth Grandmother, a shamanic spirit that resides in the inner room or houswife's room and oversees conception, gestation, birth and lactation.

sanggam: An inlaying technique used on ceramics

sangmin: The peasantry (farmers, artisans, shopkeepers), one of four classes into which Chosŏn society was strictly divided.

sangsoe: The leader of a farmers' band (*nong-ak*)

sangt'u: A man's topknot

sanjo: Literally meaning "scattered melodies," it is an improvised solo instrumental form usually played on *kayagŭm* (12-string long zither) and accompanied by *changgo* (hourglass drum); a piece consists of six movements.

Sanshin: Mountain Spirit, a shamanic deity

sarangbang: The main room of the men's quarters *(sarangch'ae)* in a traditional upper-class Korean house where the master of the house studied and received guests

sarangch'ae: The men's quarters in a traditional upper-class Korean house

sari: Sarira, small mineral-like droplets that are sometimes found among the cremated remains of Buddhist monks and other religious practitioners. In Buddhist countries, they are considered an indication of spiritual maturity and are frequently enshrined and worshiped as sacred relics.

satpa: A 2-foot-long cloth with which a *ssirŭm* (Korean-style wrestling) wrestler binds his loins and upper right thigh; the wrestler grasps his opponent's *satpa* in the right hand at the loins and in the left hand at the thigh to wrestle.

sebae: A traditional New Year's custom to pay respect to one's elders by giving a deep bow

sebaetton: The money (*ton*) children are customarily given on New Year's when they do a deep bow, called *sebae*, to their elders.

shibiji: The 12-year cyclical zodiac used throughout Asia.

shijin: Observation of the face and overall appearance of the person, one of four methods of physical examination used in traditional healing.

shijip kada: Literally meaning "go to one's in-laws' house," the phrase is used to refer to a woman getting married.

shijo: 1) A three-line poetic form popular with the literati of the Chosŏn period (1392-1910)
2) The singing of *shijo* poems

shillok: Official chronicle of a monarch's reign

Shimudo (*Ox Herding Paintings*): A set of paintings illustrating the stages of spiritual progress toward Buddhahood or enlightenment

shinawi: The instrumental musical accompaniment for shamanic ritual dances

shinju: A wooden ancestral tablet, the tangible object of veneration in certain ancestral rites

shipchangsaeng: Ten (*ship*) animals, plants and objects that symbolize longevity—rocks, mountains, water, clouds, pine trees, the Fungus of Immortality (*pulloch'o*), tortoises, deer, cranes, and the sun

shipkan: The Celestial Stems, a set of ten Chinese characters which, together with the Terrestrial Branches (*shibiji*), a set of twelve Chinese characters, are used in naming the years.

so: Panpipes used solely in ritual music performed to honor Confucius at Munmyo, Temple of Confucius; also called *pongso*, phoenix pipes, because it is shaped like the wings of a bird.

sogak: Folk music; also called *minsog-ak*

sogo: Also called *maegubuk*, a small two-headed shallow drum with a wooden handle that is played with a wooden mallet; an important instrument in folk music.

sogŭm: Also called *tangjŏk*, a small transverse bamboo flute with a mouth-hole and six finger-holes

sŏkch'ŏn: The collective term for memorial rites performed to venerate Confucius and his disciples twice a year at Munmyo, the Temple of Confucius, in Seoul

Sŏkkamoni bul: Sakyamuni, the historical Buddha, Siddhatha Gautama, Sage of the Sakyas

sŏkwa: Also called *saengjin-gwa*, the lower or licentiate level examination that was part of the *kwagŏ*, the examination for appointment to public office which was first instituted by Koryŏ in 957 and continued throughout the Chosŏn period (1392- 1910)

sŏlbim: The new clothes traditionally made to wear on New Year's

sŏlchanggo: The chief percussion instrument of Korea, this two-headed drum shaped like an hourglass is known by a variety of names — *changgo*, the most commom name, *seyogo* in historical sources and *changgu* in central Korea.

Sŏn: Korean for Zen Buddhism

sŏnang dang: The shrine of a village tutelary deity

sŏng: The Korean term for surname

Sŏngju: The House Lord, the shamanic god who resides in the threshold of a house

songp'yŏn: Stuffed rice cakes shaped like a half-moon that are steamed on a layer of freshly picked pine needles, a specialty at Ch'usŏk, the Harvest Moon Festival, a time of thanksgiving

sori: The singing portions of a *p'ansori* performance

sŏwon: A private educational facility that also functioned as a shrine to renowned scholars or statesmen during the Chosŏn period (1392-1910)

soye: Calligraphy

ssirŭm: A native Korean unarmed, one-on-one combat sport involving a variety of skills including grappling, tripping and throwing

su: Water

subokch'ŏng: A storehouse for ritual implements

suin: Korean for mudra, mystic ritual gestures of the hands, signifying powers and special actions of the Buddha

sujŏ: The name by which a pair of chopsticks and a long-handled spoon used for eating are collectively referred.

sul: Liquor

sŭl: 25-string zither

sŭltae: A pencil-size bamboo stick for plucking a *kŏmun-go*, a long 6-string zither

Sumunjang: The Door Guard, the shamanistic deity who resides in the threshold of a gate

Sŭnim: Korean title of address for Buddhist monks and nuns

susal: The name by which spirit posts (*changsŭng*) are often called in the Ch'ungch'ŏng-do provinces.

sutkarak: A long-handled spoon for eating

Taeborŭm: The fifteenth day of the first lunar month, the first full moon of the year, marks the start of the farming season

taech'ŏng: A spacious wooden-floored hall in a traditional upper-class Korean house

t'aegŭk: The *yin-yang* symbol of Chinese philosophy, a circle divided into two equal parts by an S-curving line, one half being dark and the other half being light, the negative and positive principles of universal life

t'aegŭkki: The flag (*ki*) of Korea

taegŭm: Also called *chŏttae*, a large transverse bamboo flute used in both court music and folk music

Taejonggyo: An indigenous Korean religion embodying a national foundation myth whose central concept is a triune god called Hanul who embodies creator, teacher, and temporal king

taekwa: Also called *mun-gwa*, the higher or erudite level examinaion that was part of the *kwagŏ*, the examination for appointment to public office which was first instituted by Koryŏ in 957 and continued throughout the Chosŏn period (1392-1910)

t'aenghwa: Paintings of Buddhist themes that hang behind Buddhist altar figures

t'aep'yŏngso: A double-reed instrument with seven finger-holes and a thumb-hole and a large cup-shaped metal bell; also known as *soenap* and *hojŏk*, it is now used only in royal ancestral shrine music *(chongmyo-ak)*, farmers' band music *(nong-ak)* and processional music *(koch'wi)*.

Taeseji posal: The Buddhist deity Mahasthamaprapta, the Bodhisattva of Power

Taeungbojŏn: A Korean name by which the main hall of a Buddhist temple is called if it enshrines an image of Sakyamuni (Sŏkkamoni bul), the historical Buddha. *See* Taeungjŏn and Kungnakchŏn.

Taeungjŏn: The most common Korean name by which the main hall of a Buddhist temple is called if it enshrines an image of Sakyamuni (Sŏkkamoni bul), the historical Buddha. *See* Taeungbojŏn and Kungnakchŏn.

Tamun ch'ŏnwang: Vaisrana, the Guardian of the North, one of the Lokapala (Sach'ŏnwang), the Four Heavenly Kings that protect Buddhist temples by guarding the four cardinal points

tanch'ŏng: The generic name for the colorful patterns that emblazon the exposed woodwork inside and outside many traditional Korean structures; the name is derived from the Chinese characters for red and blue, its two major colors, which Koreans pronounce *tan* and *ch'ŏng*.

tang-ak: Secular music of the Chinese T'ang and Sung dynasties which, after its introduction to Korea, was altered to use in court functions.

tangjŏk: Also called *sogŭm*, a small transverse bamboo flute with a mouth-hole and six finger-holes

tang namu: A large tree in which a village tutelary deity is said to reside.

Tano: The fifth day of the fifth lunar month, a day when farmers celebrate during a lull in the busy farming season between the planting of rice seedlings and their transfer to the paddies

tanso: A small, end-blown notched bamboo flute primarily played in chamber music ensembles and also popular as a solo instrument.

t'ap: Pagoda

t'aptori: A Buddhist ritual in which a group of laymen form a ring and, led by a monk, circle a pagoda (*t'ap*) while praying and chanting sutras.

tti: A person's zodiacal animal

Togyo: Taoism

toenjang: Soybean paste, a staple of the Korean diet

t'oetmaru: A long narrow verandah with a polished wooden floor on the outside of the buildings of a traditional Korean house

tojang: A seal or chop bearing one's name that is used in place of a signature.

T'ojŏng pigyŏl (*Tojŏng's Secrets*): A book used in fortunetelling

T'ŏju Taegam: The House Site Official, the shamanic god who governs the total area within the walls of a structure and thus influences the prosperity and good fortune of all those who reside therein

tok: A ceramic storage jar, also known as *onggi* and *hang-ari*

Toksŏng: The Lonely Saint, a shamanic deity

tollimja: Also called *hangnyŏl*, it is one of the characters in a given name that indicates the bearer's generation within a clan.

ton: Korean term for money

Tong-ŭi pogam (*Exemplar of Korean Medicine*): A 25-volume medical book based on ancient Korean and Chinese treatises on medicine published in 1610

ttŏk: Rice cakes

ttŏkkuk: A rice-dumpling (*ttŏk*) soup (*kuk*) traditionally eaten on New Year's

ttŭm: Moxibustion, a traditional healing technique

t'ŭkchong: Clapperless bell struck with a mallet

t'ŭkkyŏng: Suspended stone struck with a mallet

tŭngga: The terrace orchestra, one of two orchestras that perform antiphonally to perform Confucian shrine music and royal ancestral shrine music

udo kut: A style of farmers' music and dance (*nong-ak*) performed in the coastal areas of the southwest part of Korea.

um: Korean for *yin*, the negative or passive in Chinese cosmological thought

ŭmnyŏk: The lunar calendar

ŭm-yang: The *yin-yang* principle of Chinese cosmological thought

Wangshin: The King God, a major shamanic deity

wip'ae: Ancestral tablet

wolgŭm: A 4-string plucked lute used in Korean musical ensembles in the early Chosŏn period (1392-1910) but is no longer used.

yak: Three-hole end-blown bamboo flute

yakhŏnshik: An engagement ceremony

Yaksayŏrye bul: Bhaisajyaguru, the Buddha of Medicine

yakshik: Steamed glutinous rice flavored with sugar, sesame oil, cinnamon, chestnuts, pinenuts and jujubes.

yang: Korean for *yang*, the positive or assertive in Chinese cosmological thought

yangban: The members of the two orders of officialdom who served in the bureaucracy of the Chosŏn Kingdom (1392-1910); the term came to be used for the class priviledged to hold civil and military posts in the bureaucracy, the literati or aristocracy.

yanggŭm: The only traditional instrument with strings made of steel, it is believed to have been introduced to Korea in the eighteenth century; now used only in mixed ensembles for aristocratic music.

yangnyŏk: Literally meaning "solar calendar," the term refers to the Gregorian calendar.

yesŏ: An ornate style of calligraphic writing

yŏlle-ak: Music performed at court banquets

yŏmbul: The recitation of Buddhist sutra to the accompaniment of a hand-held wooden gong or drum called *mokt'ak*

yŏn: Kite

yŏnae kyŏlhon: Marriage resulting from courting and falling in love as opposed to arranged marriages (*chungmae kyŏlhon*)

yonggo: A shallow two-headed barrel drum, usually decorated with a dragon (*yong*), played in processional music (*koch'wi*) and as an accompaniment for *p'ansori* (folk narrative singing).

Yongshin: The shamanisc Dragon God, the ruler of waters

yŏnnalligi: Kiteflying; kite is *yŏn*

Yugyo: Confucianism

yundal: An extra month that is intersperced in the lunar calendar every three years

yuso: A long rope-like decoration made of many knot configurations (*maedŭp*) and generally ending in a tassel

yut: A game played by two people or teams; it requires four wooden sticks, a game board amd markers; the object is to move one's four men around a diagram of twenty dots before the opponent; moves are determined by the toss of the sticks